T0323802

On Immigration and Refugees

'Makes the case meticulously...a terrible indictment of modern British immigration policy.'

— The Economist

'Passionately argued and shot through with a sense of urgency... an invigorating read.'

— The Tablet

'Acutely spots a blank in the mentality of earlier political philosophers who "have seldom asked what obligations a state has towards those who are not its citizens", and argues powerfully against those who "hold that we have at most only negative duties towards strangers: that, for example, we may not kill them, but have no duty to protect them from being killed."'

— The Evening Standard

'A lucid philosophical discussion of the ethical principles at stake in matters of immigration and asylum, and a sharp review of the historical ways they have been manhandled.'

— New Left Review

'Its greatest contribution is to demolish the arguments used by politicians and the media, and to expose their implicit racism... It would be hard to find another short book which analyses the causes and development of racism so clearly, and shows the connivance in fostering racial prejudice of successive governments of all parties.'

— Local Government Studies

The philosopher Michael Dummett was one of the sharpest and most prominent commentators and campaigners for the fair treatment of immigrants and refugees in Britain and Europe. *On Immigration and Refugees* was the only book he wrote on the topic and among one of the most eloquent and important reflections on the subject to have been published in many years. Exploring the confused and often highly unjust and racist thinking about immigration, Dummett questions the principles and justifications governing state policies, pointing out that they often conflict with the rights of refugees as laid down by the Geneva Convention. With compelling and often moving examples, he points a new way forward for humane thinking and practice about a problem we cannot afford to ignore.

This Routledge Classics edition includes a new Foreword by Sarah Fine.

Sir Michael Dummett (1925–2011) was Wykeham Professor of Logic at the University of Oxford. He was knighted for his 'services to philosophy and to racial justice' in 1999. His pathbreaking books on the philosophy of language and mathematics made him one of the most significant British philosophers of the last century and he was a leading campaigner for racial tolerance and equality.

"Routledge Classics is more than just a collection of texts...it embodies and circulates challenging ideas and keeps vital debates current and alive."

— *Hilary Mantel*

The Routledge Classics series contains the very best of Routledge's publishing over the past century or so, books that have, by popular consent, become established as classics in their field. Drawing on a fantastic heritage of innovative writing published by Routledge and its associated imprints, this series makes available in attractive, affordable form some of the most important works of modern times.

For a complete list of titles visit:
https://www.routledge.com/Routledge-Classics/
book-series/SE0585

Michael
Dummett

On Immigration and Refugees

With a new Foreword by Sarah Fine.

 London and New York

Cover image: Ruslanshug / Getty Images

First published in Routledge Classics 2024
by Routledge
4 Park Square, Milton Park, Abingdon, Oxon OX14 4RN

and by Routledge
605 Third Avenue, New York, NY 10158

Routledge is an imprint of the Taylor & Francis Group, an informa business

First published 2001 by Routledge

British Library Cataloguing-in-Publication Data
A catalogue record for this book is available from the British Library

ISBN: 978-1-032-64165-2 (hbk)
ISBN: 978-1-032-64162-1 (pbk)
ISBN: 978-1-032-64168-3 (ebk)

DOI: 10.4324/9781032641683

Typeset in Joanna
by codeMantra

To Ian Martin

CONTENTS

FOREWORD TO THE ROUTLEDGE
CLASSICS EDITION

'At the invitation of Routledge and the series editors,' wrote
Michael Dummett in his preface to *On Immigration and Refugees*
(2001), 'I have tried in this book to bring together two things
that interest me: philosophy and the politics of race, something
I had never thought of doing before' (p. xxiii). In that case, we
owe a sizable debt of gratitude to Routledge and the series editors. As anti-racist campaigner Ann Dummett—Michael's wife
and some-time co-author—put it, 'his contribution is surely
unique'.[1]

Professor Sir Michael Dummett FBA (1925–2011) retired
from his position as Wykeham Professor of Logic at the University of Oxford in 1992. Described by Ray Monk as 'one of
Britain's most influential 20th century thinkers', Dummett was
internationally renowned for his research in the philosophy
of language, philosophy of mathematics, logic, metaphysics,

and the history of philosophy.[2] He was an authority on the work of Gottlob Frege (1848–1925). Dummett's magnificent philosophical reputation lives on in the discipline. However, younger generations of philosophers often are surprised to hear that Dummett was no less a towering figure in British anti-racist politics. He was knighted in 1999 for 'services to Philosophy and to Racial Justice'.[3]

Dummett was distressed to discover that Frege, the philosopher whose work he most revered, subscribed to views he most abhorred. In his book, *Frege: Philosophy of Language* (1973), Dummett noted: 'there is some irony for me in the fact that the man about whose philosophical views I have devoted, over years, a great deal of time to thinking, was, at least at the end of his life, a virulent racist, specifically, an anti-Semite.' By contrast, learning about Michael Dummett's life is a joyful, inspiring experience. I never had the pleasure of meeting Dummett, and the more I come to know about him, the more I admire him. And whereas Dummett thought he could assess Frege's philosophical contribution in isolation from his racist views, I think some knowledge of Dummett's life and his participation in the struggle against racial injustice is vital for appreciating the importance of his contribution in *On Immigration and Refugees*.

Dummett's passions permeate the book. He was a devout Roman Catholic (he converted in 1944 at the age of 19) and published widely on Catholicism. While he does not make explicit reference to his Christian faith in *On Immigration and Refugees*, the text is peppered with Christian examples of compassion, charity, and hospitality. He mentions Christ's story of the Good Samaritan (p. 43); he argues that Pope John XXIII 'came close to endorsing the principle of open borders' (p. 47); he highlights the Old Testament demand for humane treatment of strangers (p. 81); and he discusses the case of a government minister vowing to deport a family just before Christmas, noting that 'not one newspaper made the obvious comment about room at the inn' (p. 94). In a later interview, he made the connection explicit. Reflecting on whether there might be a tension between his philosophical work and his social justice work, Dummett answered, 'there wasn't a tension between my work against racism and philosophy, they're both very much connected in my own feeling with my religion. I think that it's a duty to help the poor and oppressed if you can, and that springs very much from, or I mean is a consequence of, a Christian view of the world'.[4] The arguments in *On Immigration and Refugees* cohere with those commitments. First and foremost, it is a book of great decency and humanity.[5]

Those well acquainted with Dummett remark upon his devotion to his family.[6] Dummett described Ann as 'my constant support and delight throughout my life'.[7] They had seven children, of whom two died in infancy. In *On Immigration and Refugees*, Dummett is especially attentive to the harms that aggressive anti-immigration attitudes and harsh immigration controls inflict upon children and families. In a memorable passage, he recounts an incident from 1976, following the decision of the Malawian President to expel all residents of Goan descent. Two families—'citizens of the UK and colonies'—arrived in Britain 'with several small children, bereft of all their money and possessions'. Dummett recalls 'watching BBC television with incredulity while it showed a BBC reporter browbeating the bewildered family with the question, "Have you come for British welfare handouts?"' (p. 105). He calls for sympathy and compassion for people who move because they are unable to feed their children (e.g. pp. 43, 122).

A man of many talents, Dummett published influential work on theories of voting and social choice.[8] He was also a leading expert on Tarot card games. We see traces of both interests here. In his discussion on democracy and representation, he emphasises the importance of voting system selection (pp. 12–13).

In addition, he writes that egalitarians believe states have a duty to 'correct for inherited inequalities as much as can be done, as in a card game which awards a premium to a player for having no trumps or no court cards in his hand, or gives the victory to one who wins no tricks' (p. 23).

While the aforementioned themes are implicit, Dummett's express aim was to combine his work in 'philosophy and the politics of race'. The book is divided into 'Part 1: Principles', and 'Part 2: History'. That might give the (in my view, mistaken) impression that the first part is properly 'philosophy', whereas the second is not. Indeed, it seems that Dummett himself was under that impression—he wrote, 'I consider that Part 1 of that book is a work of philosophy' (with the implication that he didn't think the same was true of Part 2).[9] On his intentions for Part 2, Dummett explained: 'Many people...do not understand how we in Britain got to where we are: in particular, they do not realise how deeply rooted in the history of British racism are today's attitudes to asylum seekers. I believe it is important for these things to be understood...' (p. xxvi). Those aspects of the story very much inform Dummett's philosophical treatment of migration and are the key to grasping Dummett's lasting contribution. His is a distinctive, respected voice on the subject precisely because of his first-hand interactions with the oppressive system. That 'understanding of the pervasiveness of racism', as Robert Bernasconi explains, 'came as a direct result of [the Dummetts'] sustained contact with those who were suffering directly from it.'[10] In short, Dummett's practical understanding of the workings of racism and his philosophical approach to questions about racism and migration existed in a symbiotic relationship.

Dummett served in the British armed forces from 1943 to 1947, originally in the Royal Artillery and then in the Intelligence Corps. Eventually he was sent to (what was then) Malaya.

He thought that his 'passionate hatred of racism' had originated in Malaya.[11] There he witnessed myriad ways—better pay, different forms of travel, exclusive membership clubs—in which 'the British masters of pre-war colonial Malaya had maintained and acted out the myth of white racial superiority'.[12] That experience of racist colonialism impressed itself upon him, and its influence is evident in these pages. In the book's preface, Dummett also mentions other formative experiences, including his visits to the United States in the 1950s and 1960s, during which he joined the N.A.A.C.P., had a 'personal meeting' with Dr Martin Luther King (and saw Billie Holiday sing), and encountered 'total segregation' in Montgomery.[13]

It bears repeating that in 1964 he and Ann determined to devote themselves to the fight for racial justice in Britain. He co-founded the Oxford Committee for Racial Integration, which affiliated to the Campaign Against Racial Discrimination (C.A.R.D.), and through this work he became involved in immigration-related activities. At a time when immigration officials could refuse entry to people arriving at the airport, he took it upon himself to intervene regularly and 'make representations' on behalf of people facing refusal—and he was often successful (p. xxiv). For Dummett, the fight for immigration justice was always part and parcel of the fight for racial justice. He was one of the founders of the Joint Council for the Welfare of Immigrants (J.C.W.I.). Dummett explained that, when setting up J.C.W.I., 'we chose immigration as the sector to be tackled [in the anti-racist struggle]', because the call to 'stop immigration' was one of the primary ways in which racism expressed itself Britain.[14] In turn, argued Dummett, racially motivated hostility towards immigration was 'readily transmuted into national hostility towards refugees' (p. xxv).

Dummett warned the reader to be aware that 'important events are highly likely to have occurred between the writing of this preface and the publication of the book', not least because migration-related rules and regulations change so quickly (p. xxvi). Of course, countless seismic events have occurred between his writing of that preface in 2000 and my writing of this foreword over twenty years later. Most devastating are the deaths of 59,220 people on migratory routes since 2014 (as recorded by the Missing Migrants Project). That number will have risen by the time you read this. Increasingly, people and organisations who come to the aid of migrants in difficulty— for example, NGOs involved in search and rescue operations at sea—are accused of facilitating irregular migration and are being prosecuted by states, in a development that has been dubbed the 'criminalization of solidarity'. In the United Kingdom alone, we have endured the Conservative government's 'hostile environment' policies designed to make life impossible for people without regular immigration status. These policies generated the shameful Windrush Scandal, in which hundreds of Black Britons of Caribbean origin were wrongfully denied access to healthcare, lost jobs and housing, and were being detained and even deported. The UK has left the European Union, after a 'Leave' campaign which focused heavily on 'taking back control of our borders' and restricting access to asylum. A serving Home Secretary declared it her 'dream' and 'obsession' to see a 'front page of the *Telegraph* [newspaper] with a plane taking off to Rwanda', deporting asylum seekers.[15]

No doubt Dummett would have been saddened but not shocked by these developments. He will have understood better than anyone that, when it comes to the politics of migration control, *plus ça change, plus c'est la même chose*. Moreover, I expect he would have cautioned against holding out hope that things will change dramatically for the better with a change of government. He reiterated that unjust immigration policies in the UK have been introduced and retained by successive Conservative and Labour governments. In a passage that resonates a little too uncomfortably today, Dummett reminds us that, when Labour came to power in 1964, some Labour voters believed a Labour government would repeal the Conservative's Commonwealth Immigrants Act of 1962. However, 'they experienced a sorry surprise' (p. 93). That Labour government, Dummett contended, went on to commit 'the most shameful act of any British government since the war', pushing through a new Commonwealth Immigrants Bill aimed at removing the right to live in Britain from Asians in East Africa who were British citizens (p. 96).

Since the first edition of On Immigration and Refugees, some of the nomenclature concerning 'race' and migration has changed. If he were writing today, I suspect Dummett would draw a clearer distinction between 'smuggling' and 'trafficking'. We face a different set of conflicts and troubles that are prompting people to seek asylum. The policies designed to respond to those movements have different names (such as 'the Illegal Migration Act', 2023). Home Secretaries have come, wrought their damage, and gone. Ultimately, though, I am sorry to say that the trends, patterns, and harms which Dummett identified endure. His analysis remains just as pertinent two decades on. Among other things, he argued that the Refugee Convention definition of refugees is 'too restrictive', but worried about the risks of trying to alter the Convention, since 'there are many signatory states that now consider its terms too generous' (p. 35); he highlighted the cruelty of incarcerating refugees in detention centres and prisons (p. 39); he pointed out that clandestine migration routes are the product of policies which make it impossible for people to move legally, and that this has deadly consequences (pp. 41–42); he warned of the effects of climate change (p. 25); he noted the ways in which hostility towards refugees is incited by talk of 'bogus' asylum seekers who are '"mere" economic migrants' (p. 122); he underscored how policies aimed at making it more difficult for people to move freely across borders have the unintended effect of making people stay (p. 63); he wrote knowledgably about the precarity of irregular migrants (p. 68); he recognised that immigration officials often have a wide degree of discretion when it comes to implementing the rules, and that this introduces additional injustice into the system (p. 71); he remarked on the tendency of those demanding tighter controls to exaggerate the numbers of people likely to move (pp. 109–110); he drew attention to the ongoing persecution of Roma communities (e.g. pp. 134–135, 139); and, in a haunting and devastating forewarning, he asked whether we in Fortress Europe will 'complacently watch from our safe vantage-point great tides of would-be refugees wash about the world, turned away from one country and then another, drowning as ramshackle boats go down…?' (p. 127). 'Surely not', replied Dummett (p. 127). To our eternal shame, now we must answer in the affirmative.

Although today's politics of migration would outrage Dummett, I imagine that he would have taken comfort from developments in philosophy. When he turned his philosophical attention to the subject at the turn of the century, the philosophy of migration was nascent. Now it is blooming and booming. It has become a core feature of philosophy and political theory curricula. Dummett's book is widely cited in that literature. He engaged with a variety of questions that continue to animate the debate. For example, he reflected on the merits and limitations of the principle of self-determination (pp. 8–10). He defended what he called 'the right to be a first-class citizen' (p. 10). He made the case for duties of justice applying beyond the borders of states (p. 25). He recognised that global challenges require global actions (pp. 36–37). Throughout he drew on real world examples and situated his arguments in their political and historical context. He was principled and pragmatic (p. 34).

He argued that there should be a presumption in favour of the freedom to move, and the onus should be on states to prove that there are legitimate grounds for exclusion in any particular case. 'The principle of open frontiers ought to be accepted as the norm' (p. 70). The 'upshot' is that 'each state ought to admit those who seek to enter its territory unless one of the exceptional circumstances that would justify a refusal applies' (p. 51). So he was on the side of (generally!) open borders. He did not endorse something like a human right to international freedom of movement and nor did he entirely reject the idea of a state's right to exclude non-citizens, because he thought there are 'two rare cases' in which exclusion would be permissible: when the current residents are in 'genuine danger' of what he calls a kind of cultural 'submergence', and when there is a real threat of 'serious overpopulation' (p. 70). He was emphatic that there was no risk of these exceptional grounds applying any time soon in the kinds of large, diverse, powerful countries so determined to limit migration and keep out refugees. Instead his concern was for smaller and/or less powerful countries, such as Malaya, Fiji, East Timor, and Tibet, and was based on concrete examples of colonialism and state-sponsored aggression. Once again, we see his experiences informing his analysis: 'submergence has threatened only those ruled by imperial powers or annexed by expansionist ones' (p. 49).

I think it is fair to wonder whether Dummett would have been more sanguine about a human right to international freedom of movement and less accepting of the notion of a right to exclude had he enjoyed the opportunity to follow later interventions in the literature. For example, as Kieran Oberman points out, we do not need to think—as Dummett does—of human rights as 'absolute'. Just as it may be permissible to impose some limits on the exercise of a person's human right to move freely *within* a country when, say, a deadly virus is sweeping the globe, so it may be permissible to impose some restrictions on the exercise of an erstwhile human right to international freedom of movement when relevant grounds apply.[16]

In terms of the book's enduring legacy, Dummett must take credit for insisting on the centrality of the history and politics of racism in any critical analysis of migration control. This motivates his guiding rule: 'whatever the principles governing immigration policy should be, a first requirement for it to be just is that it should not be racially discriminatory' (p. 59). Dummett's work has been pivotal in more recent moves to situate the history and politics of racism and colonialism at the heart of debates in the philosophy of migration. In effect, I think Dummett has been instrumental in enabling the kind of work that he does in Part 2 of the book to be recognised as properly philosophical, even if he himself didn't view it like that at the time. Indeed, as Robert Bernasconi maintains, this is also true of Ann Dummett's writing on racism.[17] Bernasconi argues persuasively that the Dummetts were key early contributors to critical philosophy of race in Britain. Were Dummett writing *On Immigration and Refugees* today, I conjecture that he would have engaged with relevant, ground-breaking work in critical philosophy of race, for example by Linda Martín Alcoff, Bernard Boxhill, Charles W. Mills, and Naomi Zack. I expect he would have been delighted by recent publications on migration that are grounded in that approach.

In *On Immigration and Refugees*, we see Dummett had the philosopher of language's keen eye for the importance of linguistic practices and the significance of our choice of words. This is particularly apparent in his analysis of how 'immigrant' became a 'code-word' for 'not white' (p. 92). Recent years have seen the growth of exciting work—for example, by Luvell Anderson,

Kristie Dotson, Jennifer Saul, and Jason Stanley—combining insights from the philosophy of language, epistemology, ethics, social and political philosophy, feminist philosophy, and critical philosophy of race, to analyse propaganda, political speech, slurs, dog whistles, and forms of epistemic injustice.

Michael Dummett's *On Immigration and Refugees* continues to inspire its many, grateful readers. Though we cannot do justice here to Dummett's legacy, we can award him no higher accolade than repeating Ann's powerful words: 'he made a difference.'[18]

Sarah Fine, 2023

With thanks to Duncan Bell, Chris Bertram, David Owen, Adrian Moore, and Michael Potter for their helpful comments.

NOTES

1 Ann Dummett, 'Work Against Racism', in Randall E. Auxier and Lewis Edwin Hahn (eds.) (2007) *The Philosophy of Michael Dummett. The Library of Living Philosophers, Volume XXXI* (Chicago and La Salle, Illinois: Open Court), pp. 845–855, p. 854.

2 Ray Monk, 'Gottlob Frege: The Machine in the Ghost', *Prospect*, October 2017.

3 See Daniel Isaacson and Ian Rumfitt, 'Michael Anthony Eardley Dummett', *Biographical Memoirs of Fellows of the British Academy*, XVII, 2018, pp. 191–228, p. 193.

4 Rudolf Fara, Maurice Salles, and Michael Dummett, 'An Interview with Michael Dummett: From Analytical Philosophy to Voting Analysis and Beyond', *Social Choice and Welfare*, volume 27, number 2, pp. 347–364, p. 13.

5 As Kwame Anthony Appiah agrees in 'Immigrants and Refugees', in Auxier and Hahn, *The Philosophy of Michael Dummett,* pp. 825–840, p. 828.

6 See for example Isaacson and Rumfitt, 'Michael Anthony Eardley Dummett', and A.W. Moore, 'Sir Michael Dummett Obituary', *The Guardian*, Wednesday, 28 December 2011.

7 Michael Dummett, 'Intellectual Autobiography', in Auxier and Hahn, *The Philosophy of Michael Dummett,* pp. 3–32, p. 10.

8 For further discussion of this aspect of Dummett's work, see Fara et al. 'An Interview with Michael Dummett'.

9 Michael Dummett, 'Reply to Kwame Anthony Appiah', in Auxier and Hahn, *The Philosophy of Michael Dummett*, pp. 841–844, p. 844.

10 Robert Bernasconi, 'Theorising and Exposing Institutional Racism in Britain: The Contribution of Ann and Michael Dummett to Critical Philosophy of Race', *Journal of Applied Philosophy*, volume 34, number 4 (2017), pp. 593–606, p. 596.

11 Dummett, 'Intellectual Autobiography', p. 8. But see Isaacson and Rumfitt, 'Michael Anthony Eardley Dummett', p. 194 for a suggestion that his staunch anti-racism predated his Malaya experience.

12 Dummett, 'Intellectual Autobiography', p. 8.

13 Dummett, 'Intellectual Autobiography', p. 13.

14 Dummett offers a more detailed account in his 'Intellectual Autobiography', pp. 22.

15 Lizzie Dearden, 'Suella Braverman Says It Is Her "Dream" and "Obsession" to See a Flight Take Asylum Seekers to Rwanda', *Independent*, Wednesday, 5 October 2022.

16 See Kieran Oberman, 'Immigration as a Human Right', in Sarah Fine and Lea Ypi (eds.) (2016) *Migration in Political Theory: The Ethics of Movement and Membership* (Oxford: Oxford University Press), pp. 32–56.

17 Bernasconi, 'Theorising and Exposing Institutional Racism in Britain', pp. 596–597.

18 Ann Dummett, 'Work Against Racism', p. 853.

PREFACE

At the invitation of Routledge and the series editors, I have
tried in this book to bring together two things that interest
me: philosophy and the politics of race, something I had never
thought of doing before. From 1950 to 1992 I devoted myself
professionally to philosophy, teaching it and writing about it.
I have continued to write and lecture about it since my retirement in the latter year. But I have had for all my adult life an especial loathing of racial prejudice and its social manifestations.
After some little experience of these on visits to the United
States – I was in Montgomery, Alabama, in 1956 during the bus
boycott which first brought Dr Martin Luther King to national
prominence, and was a rank-and-file member of the Congress
On Racial Equality on visits to California – in 1964 I became
involved, together with my wife Ann, in the struggle against
racism in Britain. For four years I devoted every minute that I
could spare to that struggle; I carried out my teaching duties,

but abandoned all attempt at creative work in philosophy. The affiliation to the national Campaign Against Racial Discrimination (CARD) of the local group of which I was co-founder – the Oxford Committee for Racial Integration (OCRI), whose first paid officer my wife later became – brought me into CARD and soon on to its executive committee.

It was more or less accidental that I became particularly involved with immigration. At that time the entry clearance system was not in operation: people arrived at Heathrow from the Caribbean or the Indian subcontinent, and were summarily put back on the next returning plane if the immigration officer refused them entry. It was, however, possible to intervene to 'make representations' on behalf of anyone refused entry if one could do so before the person was put on the plane. It was also sometimes possible to get a decision reversed after the person refused had arrived back where he had started: my wife, acting on behalf of OCRI, succeeded after many months in doing this for a young boy who had arrived on his own and had been sent back on his own on the basis of false information supplied by the Oxford police. Local community groups from all over the country were sometimes able to intervene when their members were expecting relatives; but the system was very haphazard, and many people were sent home without having anyone to make representations for them. Acting in the name of CARD, I set up an unofficial network of informants at Heathrow who would telephone me, at any hour of the day or night, when they heard of someone's being refused. I had then to telephone the Chief Immigration Officer, and tell him, when at last I got through, that I wished to make representations; next I had to dash to the airport, find out the background facts and make my representations to the immigration officer. Remarkably, these were often successful; but the system was still haphazard, and very disruptive of my teaching work.

In the autumn of 1967, after months of preparatory work visiting local organisations all over the country, in which I took a large part, we held the founding meeting of the Joint Council for the Welfare of Immigrants (JCWI). The purpose was to unite local and national organisations for a twofold purpose; about 200 of them affiliated at the inaugural meeting. One of the aims was to carry out casework on behalf of intending immigrants threatened with refusal and those already settled experiencing difficulty in getting their families allowed to join them, and so plug the gaps in the haphazard arrangements hitherto existing. The second objective was to campaign against the injustice of the immigration laws. CARD itself virtually collapsed at the end of 1967: JCWI continues to flourish. I became its first Vice-Chairman, and was later Chairman for some time. I am still connected with it as Trustee, and remained on its executive commitee for a great many years.

By chance in the first instance, my work in the collaborative effort to combat racism had come to concern the very wellspring of British racism. Turning the screws ever tighter and tighter against the entry of immigrants – always understood as 'coloured' immigrants – was the racists' demand and the politicians' code signal that they sympathised with them: it could easily be read as saying, 'We don't want those people here'. It was readily transmuted into national hostility towards refugees, and a tough policy towards them. A detailed account of the whole process is given in Part 2 of this book.

Apart from two essays I have written about nuclear deterrence, my work in philosophy has mostly lain far away from its social, political and moral sectors: it has chiefly concerned logic, the philosophy of mathematics, the philosophy of language and certain parts of metaphysics. I have sometimes been asked whether it was my philosophical views that had impelled me into participating in the struggle against racism, but this has not been so at all; I have a general belief that it is the duty of intellectuals to engage in any matter of social importance to which they see that they can contribute, but philosophy has not driven me in this respect any more than it has driven my wife, who until her recent retirement has devoted her whole career, in one capacity and another, to the same objective, but has no interest in philosophy whatever. But, when invited by Routledge to write a volume looking at immigration and asylum with a philosopher's eye, I found the idea attractive. I have attempted, in Part 1 of this book, to formulate and justify general principles governing the matter. Most of the philosophy I have written in the past has been addressed primarily to other philosophers. This book is not. I have written for the general reader; there is no technical discussion using terms of art familiar only to philosophers: all is comprehensible to any reflective person. I hope nevertheless that the argument is rigorous.

Many people – above all, those much younger than myself – do not understand how we in Britain got to where we are: in particular, they do not realise how deeply rooted in the history of British racism are today's attitudes to asylum seekers. I believe it important that these things be understood, and have, for that reason, devoted the first two chapters of Part 2 of the book to explaining them. The last chapter offers an impressionistic account of the situation in other countries of the European Union. Readers must be warned that in every country of Europe, and in the Union itself, policy towards immigration and refugees, and the laws and regulations applying to them, change so rapidly that any book on the subject is bound to be out of date by the time it appears in print. The provision of up-to-date factual information is of course not a major aim of this book; but readers ought to be aware that important events are highly likely to have occurred between the writing of this preface and the publication of the book.

Oxford, July 2000

Part 1

PRINCIPLES

1

SOME GENERAL PRINCIPLES

What principles have governed the policies of successive British Conservative and Labour governments since the Second World War towards immigrants and refugees? And what principles have governed the policies advocated by the British media during that period towards immigrants and refugees? The newspapers, with only occasional partial lapses into decency, have acted upon a very simple principle: identify a fairly widespread prejudice, pander to it and inflame it, in the process misleading or actually lying to the readers as far as can be safely done. The objective aimed at in following this principle has of course been to increase the circulation of the newspapers and, likewise, the numbers of people listening to or watching the broadcast programmes. This is of course a hostile description: but no lover or servant of the British media could make a case that I have distorted the facts. The principle governing the policies of the Conservative and Labour governments, and indeed,

DOI: 10.4324/9781032641683-2

with a very few honourable exceptions, of all Conservative and Labour politicians, has been exactly the same. The objective, in this case, has been to maximise electoral support: to gain votes. This, indeed, has always been the principle on which British governments have acted in respect of would-be immigrants and refugees. It had emerged in the Aliens Act of 1905, designed principally to keep out European Jews, and the Aliens Restriction Act of 1914 and the Aliens Restriction (Amendment) Act of 1919, designed to keep out Germans. Reflection on these and other capitulations to and encouragement of real or supposed illiberal popular sentiment may prompt reflection on how to achieve a democratic system under which the representatives of the electorate were not motivated, or at least were less motivated, by the desire to gain votes in the next election; but this problem will not be discussed here.

So long as the present political system endures, there is a great danger that British immigration and refugee policy will continue to be based on this unworthy principle alone. It is not a principle that will commend itself to any political theorist. It is a pressing matter, and of at least theoretical interest, to enquire what principles ought to inform a country's policy towards would-be immigrants and refugees so long as it retains untrammelled control over their admission. Indeed, reflection on this question, if the British public could be induced to engage in it, might sufficiently alter public attitudes so as to affect the dispositions of politicians to try to appease the assumed public hostility to the admission of anyone we have the power to turn away.

The first question is on what the identity of a state should be founded. This is relevant, because the state may choose freely to admit a potential immigrant who shares the identity by which it defines itself. Israel, for instance, identifies itself as a Jewish state, and on this ground operates the law of return, under which anyone who qualifies as a Jew is guaranteed admission and settlement. Another example is Germany, which still in part identifies itself by ethnic descent: all people of demonstrably German ancestry, no matter how remote, such as those who emigrated to Russia generations ago, are assured of admission to the homeland, at least if they are deemed to partake of German culture. Equally, a state may choose to exclude those who do not share the identity it ascribes to itself: the White Australia policy, now for some decades abandoned, refused admission to anyone other than those of white European descent. Conversely, the constitution of Malawi denies citizenship to anyone not of black sub-Saharan race. Thus nationality or race may be treated as part of a state's identity, so that those not of the right race or descent are to be denied entry, residence or the ultimate certification of belonging, citizenship. Again, the identity of a state may be founded upon a particular religion, as is that of all those countries designating themselves 'Islamic Republics'. This was true of almost all European countries during the Middle Ages and for some centuries afterwards: they proclaimed themselves to be Christian kingdoms; after the schism, to be Catholic or Orthodox kingdoms; after the Reformation, to be Catholic, Orthodox or Protestant kingdoms or republics. As being Christian states, they took for granted their right, when they wished, to expel Muslims or Jews. Israel is a mixed case. To be a Jew and so claim admission under the law of return, one must prove birth from a Jewish mother: the criterion is racial. The claim is not invalidated by failure to practise the Jewish religion or even by overt renunciation of it; but the criterion is in part religious nevertheless, because adherence to any other religion is held to invalidate the claim. Language may be seen as essential to a state's identity: Mussolini endeavoured to suppress the use of French or German by inhabitants of Italy, even though the country contains numerous people whose languages those are; and in our own day Turkish governments have forbidden the use of Kurdish. In both cases, even schoolchildren have been prohibited from using their mother tongues, not just in classrooms, but in playgrounds.

We may admire those mediaeval states, such as Sicily under the Normans and, in the earlier periods, Spain under the Abbasids, which practised religious tolerance. But we cannot with assurance condemn those which made religion integral to their identity. The world at the turn of the twentieth century is one in which there has long been no possibility of crossing any but a very few frontiers unhindered, but in which travel is swifter and easier than ever before, and there are manifold calamities – persecution, violence, war, hunger – pressing people to flee the lands in which they are living. We can therefore say with assurance that, in the world as it now is, and as it will doubtless be for many centuries yet, no state ought to take race, religion or language as essential to its identity. If it does, it will inevitably find living within its borders minorities not of the favoured race, practising religions other than the favoured one, speaking languages different from the majority tongue. These minorities will be liable to persecution or discrimination, whether by the laws of the state itself or by the actions of those who belong to the dominant group (usually, but not always, the majority). Whether or not such discrimination is severe, members of these minorities will feel themselves to be 'second-class citizens', when they are allowed to be citizens at all. However much they would like to do so, they will feel unable to identify themselves whole-heartedly with the country to which they belong: Christians will be constantly reminded that it is an Islamic state to which they owe allegiance, or Muslims will constantly have recalled to them 'our Christian traditions'. There is no country in today's world that does not have racial, religious or linguistic minorities; even if it lacked them, they would soon arrive.

A self-governing nation indeed needs an identity; and this identity will always be in part informed by its history. But what is 'its' history? The way in which English history has for a long time been taught in England gives one answer to this, preferable to most others. English history has traditionally been taught in an imperialistic and triumphalist fashion, but in one respect the tradition of teaching it has been admirable: it has been taught as the history of a *land*, not of a *people*. As taught in schools, it used to begin with the Romans; after the Romans left, they were ignored in favour of the Britons left behind. The Angles, Jutes and Saxons arrived: they sprang into existence, as it were, when they invaded the land; no one cared what they were doing before that. Much the same has been true of the Danes and, later, of the Normans; few English schoolchildren ever grasp the extent of Canute's realm, or even hear that other Normans conquered Sicily. This contrasts notably with the way in which history is taught in Turkey. Turkish children are indeed taught the history of Anatolia, but the primary emphasis is on the history of the Turkish people, from its origins in central Asia long before the conquest of Asia Minor.

But the identity of a state cannot be grounded solely in the territory over which its dominion extends. If it is not to be grounded in a common ethnicity, religion or language, it must be grounded in shared ideals, a shared vision of the society it is striving to create. If these are not wholesome, they will sooner or later be overturned: neither the Italian Fascist vision nor that of Nazi Germany could supply a sense of identity that would endure for very long. The Fascist vision was never one shared by the whole Italian people; even had Germany won the Second World War, the Nazi vision could not endure because it was racist to its core, and could not be shared by the subjugated European peoples. There is no need for the ideals to be representable as having been handed down from the immemorial past. After a revolution, a nation adopts new ideals as binding it together, as did the first French Republic; if the nation's history has taken an evolutionary form, there is no reason why the vision towards which it has evolved should not have taken shape only gradually. Of course, history will always play a part in defining a nation's identity; the present must be seen as having grown out of the past, but by no means as having always been there in embryo. Traditional customs, so long as they do not express a rejection of minorities – for instance, a rejection of Catholics in a predominantly Protestant land – will always exercise a binding effect.

But how can this ideal prescription be followed by every nation in today's world? Some nations were created, and some of them quite recently, in response to a demand for self-determination, or to be a home for a persecuted people or the adherents of a minority religion nervous of being persecuted: the state of Israel is an obvious example, and Pakistan another. How could such states not define themselves by race or religion? In any case, is the principle of self-determination – what was originally called *national* self-determination – entirely spurious? We have in very recent times seen that principle wreak havoc, prompting war, massacre, rape and the destruction of cities and places of worship in what was Yugoslavia. We have also seen, in East Timor, the same effects stemming from a resolute resistance to self-determination. What should we think about this principle, once so widely esteemed?

Suppose it were universally agreed that demands for independence should be adjudicated by some international body, and that all were willing to abide by its decisions. This would prevent many of the civil wars that have been fought since 1945; but on what principles should the international adjudicators base their decisions? Was it right that Bangladesh should break away from Pakistan? Would it have been wrong for Biafra to

separate itself from the rest of Nigeria? Should the divorce between Slovakia and the Czech Republic have taken place? Ought
Chechnya to be granted its independence? The principle followed in large part by the peacemakers of Versailles after the
First World War was that of national self-determination: every
nation deserves to inhabit a state exclusively reserved for it. This
was an absurdity from its first introduction; for we have no way
of saying what constitutes a nation. Do the Welsh form a nation? Do the Swiss? Or the Basques? Do Australian aborigines,
or Native Americans? Even now the state of Israel exists, we are
not disposed to call the Jews a nation, rather than a people: but
what distinguishes a nation from a people? Our propensity to
speak of a group of people as forming a nation is in large part
influenced by whether or not it has a territory of its own. We
do not count the Gypsies (Roma) as a nation, because they have
no land of their own, but are scattered through many lands.
Until the break-up of Yugoslavia, we should have been ready
to classify the Yugoslavs as a nation; now we are more likely to
speak of the Serb, Croat and Slovene nations, with some hes-
itation about Bosnians and more about Kosovars. But this in-
clination renders the principle of national self-determination
circular: if we recognise a group of people as forming a nation
according to whether it has a territory it can call its own, the
principle that a group is entitled to belong to a separate state if
it constitutes a nation is no guide at all.

But surely there is *something* in the principle of national
self-determination. Was it not an injustice that a state of Kurd-
istan was never formed? Are not the Kurds, in Turkey classified
as 'mountain Turks' and bombarded, gassed in Iraq, persecuted
everywhere, entitled now to have a country and a state of their
own? Should not Tibet be freed from the domination of the
Chinese, resolved to obliterate its culture, and have its independence recognised? Do we not rightly applaud the Greek

War of Independence, for whose cause Byron wrote his stirring lyric? Justice answers all these questions 'Yes'. What is the principle which justice follows?

The truth within the principle of national self-determination is that everyone has the right to live in a country in which he and others of a group to which he belongs are not persecuted, oppressed or discriminated against, in which his religion, language, race and culture are not reviled or held up to contempt and in which he can fully identify himself with the state under whose sovereignty that country falls. Whether that holds good of where he is living depends in part upon the conduct of that state, and in part on the behaviour of its people: it is ultimately decided by whether that individual *feels* that he fully belongs. This may be called the right to be a first-class citizen. It is the need to implement the rights of all to be first-class citizens that ought to dominate every redrawing of boundaries and every response to calls for independence. It is this need which will sometimes require the creation of new countries rather than merely the conversion of regional into national boundaries.

Of course, years of frustrated demands for independence, which may well be justified by the right to be first-class citizens, will usually generate a nationalist sentiment of the dangerous kind in those making those demands. Nationalism is dangerous when it carries with it contempt for or hostility towards other groups, regarded as the nation's enemies, and when it asks for the creation or enlargement of a nation-state whose whole identity will be that of the nation, identified by language, race, religion or some combination of these. A state imbued with such nationalism will of course deny to any minorities within its domains a sense of belonging; even if they are not actively persecuted or discriminated against, which they probably will be, they will be firmly given to understand that, not being members of the nation, they are no more than tolerated, and are present only on sufferance. Nationalism should be sharply distinguished from a just yearning for freedom from oppression and contempt: it itself breeds oppression of and contempt for others; it provokes new nationalisms in reaction.

The right to first-class citizenship entails the right to what is called 'self-government': it rules out imperialism. An unfashionable view which is nevertheless sometimes expressed is that people have a right to be governed well, but that, granted that they are governed well, they can have no legitimate objection to whoever it is that governs them. This contention is unimaginative. The mere fact that authority resides in a class of foreigners suffices to humiliate all those subject to that authority by making them feel themselves to be second-class citizens in their own land. Given a regime with a basic democratic structure, that is, one in which the populace has, at specified intervals, the right to vote on the composition of the legislature and of the executive, the right to first-class citizenship requires that the right to vote be not restricted to some favoured segment of the population: to those of a certain race, as in South Africa under apartheid or the southern states of the US under segregation, or to those with property, as in Britain before manhood suffrage, or to males, as in Britain – and in Switzerland – before universal adult suffrage. (The denial of voting rights to children obviously does not infringe the right to first-class citizenship.)

Does self-government actually entail democracy? As we well know, a democratic system can coexist with manifold injustice: with savage inequalities of wealth and opportunity, with oppression of minorities and with endemic corruption on a grand scale.

This is partly, but far from wholly, due to a widespread misunderstanding of what democracy should be taken to be. Authority must indeed be based on the consent of the governed: but how is the will of the people to be determined?

The question ought to be addressed in deciding what voting system to adopt (and, equally, how referenda should be conducted). Very often debates about electoral systems concentrate upon the *consequences* of one system or another: does the system encourage a multiplicity of political parties, does it favour coalition governments? Consequences are undeniably important, but, before they are considered, the questions of principle must be answered: what makes a candidate truly representative of the electorate? When is a decision truly responsive to the opinions and wishes of the voters? The problem is a general one, not restricted to methods of electing members of parliament or to the conduct of national referenda: given even a small number of people – the members of a committee, say – who have to choose between more than two options, how should the resultant of their divergent opinions and desires be decided? A common answer is that the majority view must prevail. This principle is often actually identified with democracy: remarks such as, 'We must do what the majority wants – that's democracy, isn't it?', are frequently to be heard. A variant is the plurality principle – what ought to be done is whatever more people want than want any one other thing. Democracy ought not to be defined in either of these ways if a democratic system is to be founded on justice. Whether what the majority wants should prevail depends on how oppressive it is to those who do not want it, and how oppressive what they want would be to the majority. A just democratic system would be one in which due weight would be given to the wishes and opinions of all, and in which minorities would therefore be protected and duly represented. Among existing constitutions recognised as democratic, many fall woefully short of this ideal; even the best are very rough approximations. Few voting systems are designed to realise these principles, in large part because the principles themselves are not clearly acknowledged, but also because it is not generally understood how electoral systems reflect our idea of what representatives are and how systems for voting between issues, as in referenda, reflect conceptions of what constitutes a just decision.

For all that, what is normally recognised as a democratic structure makes some acknowledgement of the principle that authority rests on the consent of the governed, and gives some sense, to all but those who feel most oppressed and deprived of a voice ever heard by the powerful, that they have a part, though very small, in deciding the policies of those who govern them. But what if the governed give their consent to an undemocratic system? There can be no objection, under suitable conditions, to a temporary consent to some such system. The conditions are that the consent is justly assessed, and that there is an effective mechanism that guarantees that the undemocratic system will really be of temporary duration, like the Roman institution of a temporary dictator, or else an effective means of rescinding the consent. But consent to an undemocratic system cannot bind indefinitely: an underlying democracy is a requirement of justice.

There is a right which opponents of immigration will rejoice to see enunciated. They should not rejoice too exuberantly, for it is of extremely limited application. It is nevertheless worth stating at the outset, lest it be overlooked among more general considerations. The right is one possessed by groups united by race, religion, language or culture: such groups have a right not to be submerged. Formulation of this principle requires the greatest precision, since the standard complaint of racists and xenophobes who object to any level of immigration that is taking place, however low it may be, is that the country is being swamped; for this reason I have deliberately chosen the word 'submerge' in place of the more emotive 'swamp'. Mrs Thatcher made the utterly ridiculous assertion that the English people and English culture – or perhaps the British people and British culture (she was not specific) – would feel themselves swamped by the proportionately tiny number of people of Caribbean or Indian origin who had entered the country. No minorities of so small a size could possibly have swamped Britain or its cultures. The culture of West Indians is very similar to the British, being to a great extent derived from it; and neither it nor any of the cultures of the Indian subcontinent is in the least dominant. Some cultures are, indeed, dominant: they exercise strong gravitational attraction even from a distance. An obvious example is the culture of the United States, which exerts a gravitational pull almost everywhere. A newspaper recently reported that in some parts of Mexico the traditional, somewhat macabre, All Souls' Day customs were being replaced by American Hallowe'en practices, complete with trick-or-treat; hardly a household in Britain is not now pestered by trick-or-treat extortions on 31 October, whereas, as a first-time visitor to the US in 1955, I was puzzled to know what 'Trick or treat' could mean. The 'received' British dialect of English is ever more closely assimilated to the American dialect. Hardly anyone in Britain now says, 'It looks as if it were . . .', for example: everyone says, 'It looks like it is . . .', which is pure American. We now mean 'maize' by 'corn' and 'a thousand million' by 'a billion'; people regularly speak of their ID – another expression I did not understand on my first visit to the United States. Every few months a new Americanism takes root. A culture can be submerged without an immigrant presence. But an immigrant presence will have only a faint, and usually beneficial, effect unless the number of immigrants is very large, or their culture powerfully dominant. British eating habits have been considerably affected by the Bangladeshi, and to a lesser extent the Chinese, presence; and there has been a slight, but invigorating, influence of the Caribbean and Asian minorities on British popular music; for the rest, British culture has evolved much as it would have done without the immigration that the lady professed to see as threatening it.

There nevertheless is such a thing as a country's being submerged by immigration. Britain would indeed be in no position to complain of being swamped, even if any real danger of its being so existed. In two former British colonies the colonial authorities positively encouraged immigration that bade fair to submerge − or swamp − the native population: in Malaya and in Fiji. In Malaya the influx of Chinese, serving to promote commerce, and on a lesser scale of Indians to work the rubber plantations, came very close to reducing the Malays to a minority in their own land. In Fiji the entry of a great number of Indians actually did render the Fijian population a minority; Fiji once contained more people of Indian than of Fijian descent, and might do so still had not so many emigrated. In Malaya the cultures neither merged nor influenced one another save in the most marginal degree; but, while colonial rule continued, the communities existed side by side with very little hostility or friction. Yet independence, even in prospect, made the demography of the country a ground of conflict. The social and economic needs of Malays and of Chinese differed: Chinese naturally wanted parity of political and economic power when independence was declared, the Malays were frightened that their interests would be overridden because they would be outvoted by Chinese and other non-Malays. This has given rise to many difficulties, and conflict between the communities, of a kind unknown in colonial times, has occasionally erupted. Almost certainly the very existence of the state of Malaysia, without Singapore but including the former British territorries in Borneo (other than Brunei), is a consequence of the imbalance between Malays and other races; no one thought of Singapore otherwise than as a part of Malaya before the formation of an independent state was at issue.

It could be argued that the admission of Chinese on a lesser scale that did not threaten the Malays with being submerged might have resulted in worse evils. The Chinese in Indonesia are present in numbers very far from submerging the indigenous population, but are regularly targets of violent and often murderous attack at moments of political unrest. The example might be made the basis of an argument that the immigration of any one disparate group must be either insignificant or massive. A small minority, unjustly blamed for any calamity, is always liable to be victim to racist or demagogic fury, the argument would run; only a minority large enough to give as good as it gets will be immune to persecution or violence. There is some truth in this in societies that do not set their faces against ethnic hatred and conflict and lack effective control of incensed masses; to follow it as a general policy would be to admit the inadequacy of government.

Why does a nation have a right not to be submerged? Each person's sense of who he is derives from many circumstances: his occupation, his ideals and his beliefs, but also from the customs and language he shares with those about him. If he himself has immigrated to the country in which he is living, and is one of a number of immigrants from the same place, but has been made sufficiently welcome in his new country, he will think of himself as having thrown in his lot with the people of that country; but he will share with those other immigrants some customs and perhaps a mother tongue different from the native majority. He will have adapted to a large degree, adopting some of the indigenous customs and superimposing them on those he brought with him; but he will remain conscious of being a member of a minority and of identifying himself in part with that minority as well as with the country in which he has chosen to live. He may not, indeed, have chosen to leave his country, but have been driven from it by starvation or persecution. But if unable to return to his native land, he will have had at some stage to make a decision to remain where he is; and then he will have thrown in his lot with those living in the country that has given him refuge.

The children of immigrants – given an acceptance of them by the surrounding society – will think somewhat differently. They will retain some of the customs of their parents, but will regard themselves as full members of the national community into which they were born: in their eyes, that national community now embraces their customs and their culture as well as those traditional to that country. As time passes, assimilation may become complete: British descendants of Huguenot refugees may know of their ancestry, but are in every other respect indistinguishable from the rest of the population. Or it may not become complete, in which case there will simply be a segment of the population whose customs differ in certain respects from those of the majority. Immigrants and their descendants have the problem of how to fuse distinct cultural traditions within their own lives, a problem which becomes less acute for each generation. It is a problem which only they can solve, and with which it is for none but them to concern themselves; the business of others is only to leave them free and without pressure to solve it as they choose.

Most human beings feel some attachment to the place where they live; those who do not are deprived of a natural human sentiment, and are usually conscious of their deprivation. The scale on which 'place' should be interpreted may vary greatly according to the differing attachments that different individuals feel: it may be to the country in which they live, to a particular region, or, more specifically yet, to a city or town or country district. We each need to be able to feel at home somewhere; not just in some locality, but within the institutions and among the groups of those we are bound to by common endeavours and concerns. But home is where the heart is: feeling at home is more than familiarity. One feels truly at home with some environment only if one is attached to it or feels loyalty towards it; only then can one say, 'It is my home'. Such an attachment will usually lead someone to identify with the history of the locality or institution. An extreme example is illustrated by an incident at Syracuse, where, looking out over the sea, my wife asked a friend who was with us, a native of Syracuse, whether she was looking in the direction in which the Athenian fleet had arrived. 'Yes', he said, 'just over there. But we defeated them'. He was not claiming to be descended from the ancient Greek inhabitants of Syracuse, any more than an English Catholic of Italian descent is denying his ancestry when he joins in with 'Faith of our Fathers', singing, 'Our fathers, chained in prisons dark'. This is the 'we' that may be used by a member of a college or a cricket team when recalling events in which it took part before he or any of his colleagues were members; it is the 'we' of belonging.

Many people, probably most, have at least a dual identity: Catalan as well as Spanish, Welsh as well as British, Bengali as well as Indian, Syrian as well as Arab. People vary in which of their different identities, the wider or the narrower, is the more important to them, the more definitive of who they feel themselves to be. But in all these cases, the attachment is not only to a body of people with whom they share a language and a culture, but also to a land, the land where those people live. Of course, not everyone enjoys this association of land and people; not everyone can say, 'The place where I was born and where I live is where my people belong', nor even, 'The place where I came from is where my people belong'. But to those who do it is a consolation. No one needs to be a fierce nationalist in order to be happy to think that those with whom he most closely identifies himself have a place that is peculiarly theirs, whether or not it is where he himself lives or was born.

Moreover, cultures are fragile: they can be dissipated by the impact of other cultures. They vary in how robust they are, which is in part a matter of their prestige; but the culture of a people that is genuinely in danger of being submerged by an influx of people of different cultures, and particularly of people with especially robust cultures, is unlikely itself to be at all robust. That is why it is an injustice that immigration should ever be allowed to swell to a size that threatens the indigenous population with being submerged. It is very seldom that there is a genuine danger of this. It can happen, as we already noted, under a colonial regime indifferent to the wishes of the inhabitants of a territory it governs. It can happen also when a government is determined to obliterate a minority, and sets about it, not by massacre, or not just by massacre, but by systematically settling large numbers in its territory who do not share the culture of the original inhabitants. Examples from recent times are East Timor and Tibet.

It is worth while to discuss the concept of submergence, and the right not to be submerged, because they are so often illegitimately invoked by those engaged in propaganda against admitting small numbers of immigrants. In normal circumstances, that is, in countries which are neither part of a colonial empire nor under the rule of oppressive invaders, there is no danger whatever that even a relatively high level of immigration will threaten the native culture or population with being submerged. A vigorous culture will assimilate new features, to its own benefit, or ignore them if they cannot fruitfully be assimilated. When we discuss how justice bears on matters of immigration, we must acknowledge the right of every people not to be submerged. We must also reject the mendacious use, in circumstances in which it is entirely inappropriate, of the emotive concept of being swamped, in order to deny the just desires of would-be immigrants and refugees.

Should countries like Israel and Pakistan, founded as a refuge for people of a certain race or creed from actual or potential persecution, be exceptions to the principle that no modern state should define its identity by race, religion or language? No: the reasons against doing so apply as much to them as to all other countries. Their means of declaring their national identities must indeed be especially delicate. They have the right to include in them their role as a refuge for those of a particular people or faith; but they must not make membership of that people or adherence to that faith a part of what it is to belong to the nation. It is the destiny of such a nation to provide a haven for those subject, or potentially subject, to persecution on particular grounds; but it is also the destiny of that nation to create a unity from the disparate inhabitants entitled to live in that country and be its citizens, a unity founded upon common ideals of justice.

2

THE DUTIES OF A STATE TO REFUGEES

Throughout historical times, most human beings have lived within states: in tribal states, in city-states and, in the modern era, in nation-states. The state, embodied, in some periods, in the monarch, in others in the monarch in council or the like, constituted the supreme overarching civil authority over the individual. An individual might be subject to some subsidiary authority, such as a municipal government, or owe allegiance to an intermediate feudal lord; but these would be in turn subordinated to the power of the central state. Political philosophy has largely modelled itself upon this political reality: it has discussed the justification for the authority of the state, the limits to what it is entitled to do to its citizens and hence their rights against it, and the foundation of the duties of citizens towards the state and to obey its laws. Philosophers, from Plato to Rawls

DOI: 10.4324/9781032641683-3

and beyond, have enquired into the nature and foundations of justice: the definition of a just society, as well as the requirements of justice upon the actions of each individual. But they have rarely overstepped the boundaries of a society, considered as determined by the authority of a state and the scope of its laws. They have asked to what arrangements justice requires a society to conform, and what kind of laws a state may impose: they have seldom asked what obligations a state has towards those who are not its citizens, save in respect of its conduct when other states make war on it, or of its right to make war on them.

Practising the virtue of justice is an individual attribute, but justice is also a feature of a whole society, and of the authority whose laws govern that society. Plato in the *Republic* saw the attributes of individual and society as closely allied; but there is a greater distinction between the two than with any other of the virtues. The people of East Timor showed themselves brave by voting for their independence in such large numbers in the face of their enemies' threats, subsequently so savagely carried out. But their courage as a people was the sum of the courage of its members; the concept does not change when applied to a people instead of to a single person. A just society, on the other hand, is not merely one whose members act justly: it is one that functions justly as a whole.

Egalitarianism is the belief that within a just society every individual must be accorded absolutely equal treatment; this is difficult to describe, let alone achieve. Certainly it goes far beyond equality of opportunity. God deals out very unequal hands: some suffer continual illness, some enjoy robust health; some have ten talents, some five, some only one. Even complete equality of opportunity can guarantee no more than that the most gifted secure more for themselves than others do; it can still result in great disparity of wealth and power. Wealth is power. It is not just that the rich can buy more: they can force up the prices of some goods so that only they can afford them at all. For the egalitarian, it is the duty of the state to correct for inherited inequalities as much as can be done, as in a card game which awards a premium to a player for having no trumps or no court cards in his hand, or gives the victory to one who wins no tricks. For most of the past, a hierarchical vision of society was more usual: a man was due what was proper to that state of life to which it had pleased Almighty God to call him.

Those who sympathise with Nozick's writings will deny that a just society need aim at any ideal, whether egalitarian or hierarchical. In their view, natural forces of individual self-interest should be allowed to operate unchecked: it is interference with them that is unjust. If, for example, someone with a rare skill or talent is offered a huge salary for its use by those who find it commercially worth their while to pay it, he has a right to become rich by this means: to prevent him from doing so would be an injustice. (Nozick believes taxation to be unjust.)

Arguments in support of this laissez-faire view on the basis of such examples rests on a prior *presumption* that justice is only an individual virtue: that no question arises whether a whole society functions justly. We are meant to respond to these examples with a favourable judgement of the actions of the individuals involved; the employer is *entitled* to offer the large salary, if he perceives that he can profit by doing so; the talented employee is *entitled* to accept it, if the employer sees fit to offer it. Both judgements are dubious, but in any case beside the point: the question was whether a society can be just if it allows such transactions to take place unchecked. Trifling irregularities are believed to have led to the clumping of the matter of the cosmos into galaxies and clusters of galaxies. It is easy to explain how accidental advantages can lead over time to grotesque disparities of wealth and power, to the divisions of a society by class and status. Almost all societies are disfigured by such inequities: only hardness of heart or ideological dogma can blind an observer to their flagrant injustice.

Equality is the default position: deviation from it requires justification. Famously, Rawls has proposed that inequality within a society is legitimate only if the least well off sector is better off for it than it would be without it. We need not here discuss how close this formulation comes to hitting the mark. What is apparent is that we can no longer regard justice as bearing only on the functioning of a single society, considered as that comprised within a single sovereign state. The horrifying inequalities that often exist within any one such society are outstripped by the yet more horrifying inequalities between rich countries and poor ones – a disparity with the most powerful effect on migration between them. The oppression inflicted by many governments upon their peoples and the civil wars that rage in countries such as Sri Lanka account for many of the genuine refugees that flee their homelands; but the poverty that afflicts much of the Third World prompts thousands who are scorned as 'economic migrants' to seek a more bearable life in the prosperous West. The ever widening gulf between rich countries and poor countries presents the gravest problem facing the world at the beginning of the twenty-first century. Closing that gulf is the most urgent necessity that presses upon us; failure to achieve this not only maintains gross injustice, but threatens the stability of the world. So far Western political leaders have failed to recognise the urgency the problem demands, speaking blandly of overseas aid; the higher prices charged by pharmaceutical companies in the Third World instantiate the cynicism with which Western business addresses the situation. Righting the inequity requires the highest degree of political and economic skill, and perhaps the willingness of Western peoples to make sacrifices for an end they must be brought to see as compelling – and one that must be attained before global warming begins to bite hard.

Jesus's parable of the labourers in the vineyard illustrates what justice is. The owner of the vineyard hired men to work at successive times of the day, promising each of them one *denarius* for working until evening. At the end of the day, each was paid what he had been promised. Those who had worked throughout the day grumbled that they had received no more than those who had been hired later, but their employer rebuked them. The story is strikingly egalitarian: each was paid the same. Justice does not consist in giving each what he deserves – Hamlet had a sharp word for that idea: it consists in giving each his due.

There are some things which are everybody's due. The basic conditions that enable someone to live a fully human life are the due of every human being, just in virtue of being human: these are what are nowadays called 'human rights'. Ill health or other misfortunes may impede some from living fully human lives; they have the right that others, as far as lies in their power, should help them to enjoy the conditions for such lives to the best possible extent.

In international law a state has certain duties to other *states*, for instance not to invade them. To regard the human population of the world as a community of states, as a single society is a community of individuals, is clearly a false analogy: it would not matter if harm were done to a state provided that no harm were done to its citizens, if that were possible. It is plain that the duties a state has towards other states, whether enshrined in international law or not, that is, whether simply moral duties or actual legal duties, imply, and rest on, moral duties a state has towards people living outside its jurisdiction. A state ought never to invade foreign territories save under great provocation. It does not have the right to allow deforestation that will result in catastrophic flooding of its neighbours' lands; it has a duty to prohibit the emission of toxic gases likely to produce acid rain falling on the territory of others. It also has a duty, however hard to define with precision, to come to the aid of other states when disasters strike them, such as floods, earthquakes, volcanic eruptions and famine. There are a great many principles governing a state's conduct liable to affect those dwelling beyond its borders, and others determining its obligation to offer help to them in moments of sudden and severe need; these are largely unenforced and, under the existing order, outside the boundaries of possible enforcement. Here we are concerned with only one aspect: what duties and what rights does a state have towards individuals seeking to enter the land over which it rules? The initial answer has to be that it must deal with them justly: it must give them their due.

The right of the citizen of a country to live in that country, or to enter it at any time at his will, is enshrined in the UN Universal Declaration of Human Rights of 1948: no state may therefore lawfully expel or banish its own citizens. It is natural to say that someone's right to live in or enter a particular country is a mark distinguishing a citizen from a non-citizen. But to this there are well known exceptions. Any Jew has a right to enter and to live in Israel. An Irish citizen has the right to enter the United Kingdom and live there, and conversely. A citizen of a Spanish-speaking country of Latin America may freely enter Spain. A citizen of a state belonging to the European Union may enter any other member state, and remain there if he or she takes work there. Before the passing of the first Commonwealth Immigrants Act in 1962, a citizen of any Commonwealth country, or of a British colony, had an unimpeded right to enter Britain and live in it; this was a right, not of citizenship, but of British subjecthood. It would be better to say that the right to enter and live in the territory of a particular state distinguishes those who are citizens of the state, together with all others on whom that state chooses to confer that right. Sometimes it may confer the right on individuals of a particular category, the citizens of certain other countries or the members of a certain racial or religious group, but with exceptions: an EU country may refuse prostitutes, drug-dealers and terrorists coming from another EU country. But it is plain that it has no right to place limitations on the rights of its own citizens to enter or reside; and the UN Declaration recognises no such limitations. You may enter and live in the territory of the state of which you are a citizen even if you are the enemy of that state, or a threat to it.

In the later days of the Soviet Union, Western countries expressed much indignation over its practice of expelling some of its own citizens. They never declared what rights anyone so expelled should have to live elsewhere; the principle that it was the right of every state to determine who should cross its borders and who should be allowed to live in its territory was regarded as being as inviolable as the right of every individual to live in the country of his citizenship. But if everyone has the right to live in the country of his citizenship, then a fortiori everyone has the right to live *somewhere*. If it is unjust for a state to deny someone the more particular of these rights, it is unjust for other states to deny him the more general: someone unjustly expelled from the country to which he belongs by right of being one of its citizens must have a valid claim that some other country should take him in. Here we have a legitimate claim for asylum that is not recognised as such by the 1951 Geneva Convention Relating to the Status of Refugees or by most existing nation-states.

Those who have been banished from their homelands form one section of a peculiarly unfortunate category, that of those people who lack any place on the face of the globe where they have a legal claim to be allowed to go and to live. The most notorious section within this category is that of stateless people, who do not have a right to the citizenship of any state according to the laws of those states on which they might otherwise have a claim. The 1954 Convention Relating to the Status of Stateless Persons forbade any contracting state to expel stateless people lawfully resident on its territory, and required it to 'facilitate' their naturalisation; but it laid no obligation on any state to admit stateless people expelled from the country in which they were living. Another section of the category consists of those who hold some class of citizenship of some state that fails to guarantee them anywhere where they have an undeniable right to be; as is explained in Part 2, the Nationality Act now in force in the United Kingdom is particularly productive of members of this subcategory. It is plain that the creation of such classes of citizenship is an offence against a human right – the right to have somewhere where one is incontestably entitled to live; not a right as fundamental as the rights not to be murdered, tortured, raped or deprived of one's dwelling, which are those which we principally have in mind when we speak of 'human rights', and which Milosevic, Pinochet and other tyrants are accused of violating, but a right nevertheless. A similar offence against this right is the *creation* of statelessness. Not every state recognises *ius soli* – the principle that anyone born within the jurisdiction of a state is thereby a citizen of that state: Britain used to, but, since the last Nationality Act, does so no longer. Every state, even if it does not recognise *ius soli* in general, ought to include in its laws a provision whereby anyone born on its territory acquires its citizenship if the alternative would be that the newborn child would be stateless; British law before 1983 made such a provision, by recognising *ius soli*, but now allows registration as British citizens of stateless children born in the UK only under certain conditions.

But what of adults who find themselves stateless? They are plainly entitled to be granted a nationality. Simply to enunciate this principle, without saying what nationality they have the right to claim, would resemble the resolution adopted by the Congregation of Oxford University many years ago, that everyone with a University post was entitled to be a Fellow of some College, without laying down of which College any given person was entitled to be a Fellow, let alone any mechanism for enforcing the duty of that College to elect him or her. We come here upon one of many problems soluble only by international agreement. A commission ought to be established by the UN, and as many nations as possible induced to promise compliance with its adjudications. To this commission stateless persons could apply to be made citizens of some country. The commission would take into account the obvious factors: the wishes of the applicant, the languages he spoke, the location of his relatives and of others of his ethnic, cultural or religious group, the attitudes of different states towards new arrivals and their treatment of them, and so forth; when citizenship of a state signatory to the international agreement was allotted to an applicant by the commission, that state would be bound to grant him its citizenship. The success of international agreements of this sort has not been very great: the United States, in particular, is loath to sign them, and other countries, willing enough to sign, have been reluctant to comply with them. It remains that there are many current problems that can be dealt with only by international cooperation. If the nations of the world become more willing to cooperate in solving them, and more sincere in their efforts to do so, solutions will be practicable; if not, they will not be solved.

An opposite right enshrined in the UN Declaration of Human Rights is the right to *leave* one's country: a state may not lawfully erect barriers, like the Berlin Wall, to prevent its citizens from leaving. The right so proclaimed is ambiguous: is it meant to be absolute, like the entitlement of a University Lecturer to a Fellowship, or is it conditional, like the right to marry? Everyone has a right to marry, but only if someone consents to be his wife or her husband: no one has an absolute right to be married. Does one have an absolute right to leave one's country, or only a right to do so conditionally upon some other country's willingness to accept one? Most politicians would regard it as no more than a conditional right. To declare it absolute would be very close to denying the legitimacy of all immigration control, since a right to leave one's country would be nugatory unless at least some other country had the duty to take one in. An answer to this question will emerge in the next chapter.

The principle is frequently proclaimed by politicians that every state has an unrestricted right to determine whom it shall admit within its frontiers. In proclaiming it, they usually fail to make explicit mention of the exception to which they are bound by international law to which they have subscribed, the duty of a state to admit refugees, or, rather, not to send them back to the countries from which they have fled. This needs to be understood as obliging a state to which a refugee has applied for asylum not to send him or her anywhere from which he or she may be returned to that country, but only to a land where refuge will be offered. The principle is incontestably correct. Every human being has a right to refuge from persecution: to deny refuge to the persecuted is to deny them their due; it is a manifest injustice. The Geneva Convention of 1951 (to which a Protocol was added in 1966) defines a refugee as one who, having a 'well-founded fear of being persecuted for reasons of race, religion, nationality, membership of a particular social group or political opinion' is outside the country of his nationality or, if stateless, that of his habitual residence, and is unable or, owing to such fear, unwilling to return to it. The Convention thus recognises as refugees those seeking escape only from persecution, and not from any other conditions, such as famine, civil war or the impossibility of supporting oneself or one's family, which prevent someone from living a decent human life without the threat of an unnatural death. Nor does the Convention allow anyone to apply for asylum from within his own country (or, if stateless, the country of his habitual residence). It forbids contracting states to impose penalties for illegal entry on those who apply for refuge without delay. It does not lay upon them an obligation to give asylum to refugees, but only prohibits them from sending refugees back to any territory in which their lives or freedom would be threatened by reason of their race, nationality, religion, social group or political opinion; if they do not offer asylum, they must allow a refugee a reasonable time to obtain admission to another country. In practice, it is evident that, to accord with the Convention, a state must equitably examine the claim to be a refugee as understood by the Convention of anyone present on its territory who asks for asylum on that ground before deciding what action it will take. If it decides that the claimant does qualify as a refugee, it is not contrary to international law for it to agree with some other state to admit him or her, provided there is genuinely no reason to fear persecution there or danger that it will send him or her back to the country of origin. But if no other such state can be found, the state really has no option under the Convention but to admit the claimant itself.

It can hardly be claimed that either the UK or other member states of the European Union have been scrupulous in complying with the Convention's prohibition on returning refugees to the country from which they have fled. After Gypsies, the group to which European governments have been most hostile is that of Tamils from Sri Lanka. The Refugee Council in Britain and the Forum for Human Dignity in Sri Lanka have reported systematic persecution from 1998 onwards of unsuccessful Tamil asylum-seekers returned by European governments. According to the Refugee Council, those deported from Germany, France, Norway and Poland between August 1998 and March 1999 and arrested immediately upon arrival at Colombo number about a hundred. The Council gives the case history of one of these named Shanker, deported from the Netherlands in February 1998. Questioned at the airport, he was given a permit to live in Colombo, but arrested in March and again on 15 July. He was held at the police station, where he was stripped, tortured and interrogated about links with the Tamil Tigers, until 25 July. He received only one five-minute visit by an officer of the Dutch embassy during this time; European governments are eager to remove refugees, but little concerned to verify the justice of their decisions by seeing what happens when they return to their countries. Shanker was then detained for a year under the Sri Lanka Prevention of Terrorism Act, and in July 1999 released on bail, but no proper hearing has yet been held. The Forum states that those suspected of having left Sri Lanka illegally are deprived of all their documents, money and valuables. They are then detained, for hours or for weeks; not allowed to return to their homes in the north, they are often repeatedly rearrested after release. They are also often tortured in prison: the Forum has documented several cases of horrifying torture, including a man picked up, with others, off the coast of Senegal in February 1998 and a woman deported from France in October of that year.[1] The experiences of these people have shown their fears to have been very well founded indeed. Professing to subscribe to principles enshrined in international instruments is worthless if no care is taken in implementing them.

The principles embodied in the 1951 Convention are manifestly correct. That the human rights now routinely appealed to and formulated in the UN Declaration genuinely exist can be denied only by the comfortably situated and heartless. People denied the minimal conditions for a life free from terror and allowing them a basic dignity are entitled to call on others to grant them such conditions. To deny this is to hold that we have at most only negative duties towards strangers: that, for example, we may not kill them, but have no duty to protect them from being killed. This is quite false. To refuse help to others suffering from or threatened by injustice is to collaborate with that injustice, and so incur part of the responsibility for it. Hence those who are forced by fear for their lives or of torture, rape or unjust imprisonment to flee their own countries have a valid claim on other human beings to afford them refuge. Now only a state is normally in a position to accord them refuge. It would be wrong to think that, while *individuals* have such a duty towards strangers, the *state* need concern itself only with its own citizens. The state is the representative of its nationals, and acts in their name; in a democratic society, it acts at their behest. It must therefore act collectively in accordance with the moral duty laid on its citizens as individuals. It follows that the claim for refuge of those who flee from persecution should be universally recognised.

But which state has the duty of considering their claim for refuge? The Dublin Convention of 1990 (Convention Determining the State Responsible for Examining Applications for Asylum) sought to decide this question for member states of the European Community. Under it, a claim for asylum is to be considered in the first place, not necessarily by the state to which the application is first made, but by one determined by graded criteria. The first is the presence of a family member who has been recognised as a refugee and is legally resident in that state. The second is the applicant's holding a residence permit or visa to the state. The third is the applicant's having made an illegal entry from outside the EU to the state in question, unless he has been living for more than six months in another state. The fourth is a state's having admitted the applicant lawfully without a visa, unless he applies to another state to which he may go without a visa. In all other cases the application must be considered by the state to which the claim for asylum was first lodged. This Convention is intended to relieve the pressure of asylum applications upon those countries especially favoured by refugees; but it somewhat restricts the freedom of refugees to choose where they want to go. Most refugees want to return to their own countries as soon as it becomes safe to do so; at least they want to do this until they have lived so long in the country of refuge that they have come to think of it as their home. Their initial choices of where to go to apply for asylum are seldom wayward, however. They want to go where there are others of their own people, where they can speak the language or have a reasonable chance of learning it, where they will have opportunities for employment. If there is serious imbalance between asylum applications in different member states of the Union, as there usually is, a fairer solution than the rules of the Dublin Convention might be an EU tribunal for deciding to which member state each refugee should be entitled to apply for asylum, which would take into account the factors leading him to favour certain countries over others, as well as the demographic situation in those countries and their ability to provide for new entrants.

There has been gross inequity in refugee flows to different countries. The countries which have accepted refugees by the million have been the poorest ones: Pakistan, Ethiopia, the Sudan. Developed countries complain when a thousand or so arrive. It is a commonplace that the flow of refugees has greatly increased throughout the world. Probably this is also something that should be handled by international agreement. A world tribunal needs to be established by international accord, parallel to that suggested above for the European Union: such a tribunal should obviously come under the auspices of the UN High Commission for Refugees. Such a tribunal would be quite unable to consider case by individual case; but it could decide for whole categories – Tamils from Sri Lanka, for example – which countries were best fitted to consider their applications for asylum. As with all such proposals, its workability would depend upon the readiness of countries throughout the world to sign and abide by a convention to accept the adjudications of the tribunal. Again, there seems at present little likelihood of such a thing. Yet the problem of refugee flows is an international one, as are many other problems. There is little hope of an equitable solution to it save by international co-operation.

The mention of refugees to Pakistan, the Sudan and Ethiopia raises the question what entitles anyone to claim temporary asylum: for these were refugees from civil war and from starvation, categories unrecognised by the 1951 Convention on the Status of Refugees. The qualification laid down by the Convention for being entitled to claim asylum is too restrictive: all conditions that deny someone the ability to live where he is in minimal conditions for a decent human life ought to be grounds for claiming refuge elsewhere. The Convention requires revision; in particular it must be made explicit that the persecution which is offered as a ground for asking for asylum need not be persecution from state authorities: it may be persecution from others from whom the state is unable to protect them. If people are justifiably in fear of their lives, they deserve to be offered safety, whether those they are afraid will kill them are Algerian police or Islamic rebels, the Sri Lankan army or Tamil Tigers. It remains to be said that any suggestion of renegotiating the Convention is dangerous: there are many signatory states that now consider its terms too generous.

The duty of a state to accept refugees comprises a duty to consider their applications in accordance with the principles of justice, rather than in the grudging spirit now manifested by many countries anxious to reduce the number of refugees they accept to the barest minimum. In 1996 Canada allowed 82 per cent of the claims for asylum by refugees from Sri Lanka; Britain allowed 0.2 per cent. It would be an amazing accident were 99.8 per cent of such claims made to the British authorities unfounded by the same criteria that ruled out only 18 per cent of those made to the Canadian ones. In theory the criteria used in both countries *are* the same: the figures vividly illustrate the different spirits in which immigration officials of Britain and Canada exercise their subjective judgements. This does not reflect merely a difference of attitude towards the conflict in Sri Lanka: also in 1996 Britain allowed 0.4 per cent of asylum claims by Somalis, where Canada allowed 81 per cent, and 1 per cent of applications from refugees from the former Zaïre, where Canada allowed 76 per cent. However excessively lenient the Canadian officials may be conjectured to be, it is inescapable that the decisions of their British counterparts must fall very far short of justice. Many refugees whose applications are rejected by European immigration authorities are returned by them to persecution, imprisonment and torture.

The duty to accept refugees also comprises a duty to treat them with humanity while their applications are under examination, and after they have been accepted. At present it is the practice of the British Government to incarcerate numbers of refugees in 'detention centres' and in actual prisons. The excuse is that these are people liable to abscond and melt undetected into the general population. There seems little reason, however, to think that the authorities have any skill in diagnosing a propensity to do this, or even seriously attempt to do so; it is more likely, as is generally suspected, that the practice is intended as a disincentive from coming to the country and claiming asylum. The Schengen accord was signed in 1985 by France,

Germany and the Benelux countries: since then, all EU countries except the UK and Ireland have adhered to it. Its purpose is to guarantee free movement of persons between signatory countries. Other European countries have followed the British example and with the same excuse: under pressure from other Schengen countries, Italy started detaining refugees in 1998, in crowded centres where they have no facilities and no knowledge of what will happen to them. Certainly, many of those detained are quite genuine refugees: some even succeed in their asylum applications. In no case is there any excuse for treating would-be refugees in such a manner. People who have seen members of their families killed or mistreated, or who themselves have suffered terror, torture or wrongful imprisonment, need to be treated with sympathy. Placed in prison or in the near equivalent of a prison in the country from which they hoped to obtain refuge, they are driven to despair: the whole world seems to be against them. It will be replied that many of those detained are 'bogus'. The word is thoughtless. To have a claim for asylum that does not succeed is not to be fraudulent: it may be desperate or it may be optimistic, but it is not often likely to be merely dishonest.

What can motivate someone to leave his country and flee to another? It will usually be despair at the intolerable conditions in which he is living. If these do not fall within the narrow boundaries of valid grounds for acceptance of a claim for asylum, they may still be unbearable: destitution, starvation, the fear of violence, constant racial or religious abuse and harassment. Someone who feels unable to endure such conditions any longer may well hope that a country to which he escapes will recognise the depth of his misery and allow him to remain: the fact that that country is indifferent to his plight and determined to admit only those fulfilling certain narrow criteria does not make him 'bogus'.

The barriers to the entry of immigrants and refugees that have been erected by Western nations have created a traffic in illegal immigrants. Criminal organisations charge enormous sums to smuggle people into the various countries of Western Europe by clandestine and dangerous means. The horrible deaths from asphyxiation of 58 illegal Chinese immigrants startled and revolted the British public; but this was only one among many such episodes that have occurred in attempts to reach a number of Western countries. They provoke outraged denunciations of the traffickers in human beings; but the initial cause of this infamous trade is the attempt by Western governments to make it impossible for anyone from outside the EU to reach their territories. Those who successfully arrive by the routes provided by the organisers of illegal immigration normally remain illegal immigrants, heavily in debt for their passage, exploited and ill-treated. However badly deceived they had been about their chances, only something very close to despair can have prompted them to undertake such expensive and hazardous journeys.

It must be conceded that some more prudent individuals, under strong pressure, which may fall short of despair, to migrate, or even to make a short visit, perceive that virtually their only means of being admitted is to claim asylum, even if they realise that there is no chance that their claims will be accepted. These no doubt merit the epithet 'bogus'; but it is usually not they who are relegated to prisons or detention centres. For several years now hysteria about immigration has gripped most West European countries. It is exploited by right-wing populist politicians; but many politicians in the centre and on the left have succumbed to it. The result has been that severe restrictions have made it almost impossible for someone from outside the First World to get into these countries, even for a visit. This creates the strongest temptation to those who have perfectly legitimate reasons for wishing to emigrate to any such country or even just to visit it temporarily to get there by some means or other, and then to apply for asylum; even if the asylum is not granted, they cannot be removed until their applications have been considered. Draconian immigration laws encourage the unfounded applications for asylum of which those who voted in the laws then complain.

Even if a large proportion of those who apply for asylum were genuinely fraudulent, which they cannot possibly be, there would still be bound to be, among those imprisoned or detained, a substantial number who have been persecuted or tortured and have indisputable claims to be recognised as refugees. It is cruel to inflict on them a punishment that the fraudulent are thought to deserve. Compassion for those who have been subjected to real terror demands that no risk should be run of dealing with them with harshness by unexplained imprisonment: and how can that risk be avoided if asylum seekers are relegated to detention before their cases have been fully examined? Moreover, it is not the incarceration only of those with admissible claims to asylum that is cruel: to do this to people who have fled conditions they have been unable to bear, even if these do not give them claims that will be recognised by the adjudicators, is almost equally immoral.

Every state has a duty to those who flee to it for refuge from intolerable conditions. It also has a duty to help those whom it admits to settle into the country that has granted that refuge. It should provide genuine reception centres where refugees can stay if they wish, when they first arrive and until they find somewhere to live, not under lock and key or behind barbed wire, nor controlled by guards, but in pleasant conditions. At such centres there should be instruction in the language of the country and in practical matters about life there that the refugees need to know if they are to adapt to their new home.

A Home Office report issued in October 1999 shows the grievous lack of such help in Britain. Speaking of those granted refugee status or given exceptional leave to remain, it said

> Many encounter high levels of unemployment, have poor housing and health, and achieve limited access to welfare services. In addition, many suffer social isolation, discrimination and marginalisation. Social justice and human rights concerns demand that refugees should be able to live in dignity while receiving the surrogate protection of, and being in a position to contribute to, the host country. Once a refugee is granted permission to stay, there is a need to invest early in integration to promote a quick move from dependency to self-value and sufficiency.

Many are still unable to speak English; language classes are seldom provided for them by central government (the Chilean refugees who came after Pinochet's coup were an exception), although local government and voluntary agencies have helped in this way. Their past mistreatment, sometimes amounting to torture, has left many with psychological troubles which no specialist medical care is being supplied to assuage. The hostility towards them fostered by the newspapers and the consequent discrimination against them by employers combine with their language problems to force many to live on social security benefits when they could very well be usefully employed and would much prefer to be so. The neglect of their needs by the state that gave asylum is a denial of its plain duty, as well as a senseless neglect of the necessity for avoiding the social evils that spring from needlessly allowing a whole group to degenerate into a deprived and despised underclass.

If an individual has a duty to give help to those in need when they ask him for it, he also has a duty not to deny them the opportunity to ask. The same applies to states. They have an internationally recognised duty towards refugees: they therefore have a duty to do nothing to prevent refugees from reaching their borders. This duty is currently violated by almost all 'developed' states. It is violated by the imposition of visa requirements and by laws which impose heavy fines on carrying companies for bringing people without correct papers: it is rightly against international law, as embodied in the 1951 Convention, to require valid documentation from those claiming asylum, and yet British courts have sentenced some such for entering the country without genuine passports and visas. Little protest is made against these unprincipled actions: yet they are not merely contrary to justice but specifically forbidden by international law. If a country believes that it is receiving more than its fair share of refugees, it is entitled to ask other states to help it by taking some of them; it has already been observed that a formal mechanism for doing this needs to be set up. But it is not entitled to devise artificial means to prevent refugees from arriving: that is the moral equivalent of what has also often been done, turning them away unheard when they arrive.

Draconian measures to prevent or deter refugees from arriving compel those desperate for asylum to use illegal means. It is not the proper business of government to force airline officials to act as heartless immigration officers: but less regular carriers deserve to be deterred. These are the unscrupulous agents already referred to, who, for large payments, smuggle people in on unseaworthy vessels or concealed in lorries. Such agents indeed act criminally when they expose their clients to the risk of death, or charge them exorbitant fees; but indignation against them ought not to be transferred to those they exploit. No doubt one ought not to make use of the services of such agents if there is any alternative: but often there is no alternative. The combination of harsh laws to restrict immigration and the drastic measures to prevent refugees from arriving frequently means that people fleeing terrifying or intolerable conditions have no other way of escaping: the blame for the existence of these reviled traffickers in human beings lies largely with the governments that have erected the barriers the traffickers are helping frightened people to circumvent. The agents offer a service that our own government and those of other European countries have wantonly rendered necessary. Willingness to pay large amounts for those services testifies to the desperation of those who do so. They deserve compassion, not punishment. Doubtless it is right to track them down, but not in order to imprison them or return them summarily to whence they came: only to hear and consider their claims to be admitted.

But the most morally squalid of all devices to discourage refugees is to incite prejudice against them. This is very widely practised: it is particularly easy for governments to do in Britain, where they can build on an unreasoning prejudice against immigration, fostered over decades. To bring about this effect, government spokesmen constantly refer to asylum seekers in general as 'bogus' and reiterate that the great majority have unfounded claims and are therefore 'abusing the system'; this instils into the unthinking a belief that they are all dishonest and have come to the country for no good reason save that it occurred to them that they would like to live there. A favourite propaganda device is to repeat incessantly that most of the asylum seekers are mere 'economic migrants'. This phrase has the benefit of blurring the distinction between refugees and immigrants: it also serves to convey that the motives of those claiming asylum are trivial and unworthy. If you are, say, a dentist, and have left your country for another merely because dentists are paid better in the new country, then indeed any claim you make to be recognised as a refugee must be deceitful and your true motivation should command no respect – no more respect than, say, a British academic's transfer to an American university. That is what the British Government wishes the public to envisage when it employs the term 'economic migrant'. But of course to describe anyone's motive for seeking refuge in a country not his own as economic does not entail that it is so trifling. In his own country he may have been unable to feed his family; he may have seen his children die from malnutrition. It needs only a moment's thought to realise that flight for economic reasons may be as justified and as worthy of sympathy and help as flight from political persecution; but so conditioned has the British public become by unvaried official propaganda against asylum seekers that it never spares a moment to think about the question.

The manipulation of minds for unworthy ends may well be the sin against the Holy Ghost, which shall not be forgiven. Poisoning the mind of the public at large against a group of people who ask our help and deserve our pity – or, indeed, against any whole group – is a worse crime than simply treating its members unjustly. Yet the two main British political parties have colluded in it for years. When Christ reiterated the Old Testament commandment to love your neighbour as yourself, his listeners asked him, 'Who is my neighbour?'. He responded by telling the story of the good Samaritan. Is it not time for both politicians and public to ask the same question?

NOTE

1   See the *Independent*, 8 June 2000, p. 15.

3

THE DUTIES OF A STATE TO IMMIGRANTS

To recognise a state's duty to consider the claims of refugees is to reject the idea that a state has *no* duties towards those who are not its citizens. The idea that its duty is only to its citizens stems from a faulty conception of the purpose of the state's existence – its mission, in today's jargon. The reason for which the state exists is most usually said to be to promote the welfare of its citizens and to protect them against attack from without. These are among its purposes, indeed: but its further purpose is to *represent* the body of its citizens to the outside world. This is tacitly acknowledged by the personalised references to countries that occur in common locutions: when the political leaders of a country make some declaration, we say, 'Greece objects to . . .' or 'Italy agrees to . . .'. The citizens of any country have individual moral obligations to any other human beings

DOI: 10.4324/9781032641683-4

whom their actions or failures to act may affect: they therefore have, as a body, collective moral obligations to citizens of other countries. Since the state to which they belong represents them to the outside world, it has, in that capacity, moral obligations to other states and to individuals belonging to those states. In hardly any other case are we disposed to think that the obligations of an institution are to its members or clients alone. We do not think that a family, a university or a firm ought to consult the interests solely of its members. And yet it is commonplace for politicians and electors alike to think this of the actions of the state. British politicians, negotiating with other members of the European Union, are accustomed to say, 'We are doing this because it is good for Britain' or 'We shall decide whether to support or veto this according as we conclude that it is or is not in the interest of Britain': the question they should be asking themselves is whether the proposed course of action is to the benefit of the European Union as a whole.

Collective selfishness is no more admirable a quality than individual selfishness. It is collective selfishness that motivates the strident demands for national sovereignty, which usually means freedom from any supranational authority. The demand is that the national state shall be at liberty to do whatever it likes, in order to satisfy the wishes of its own members and in disregard for the rights, needs and wishes of those belonging to other countries.

Very plainly, the actions of any one country may have effects on many others, often on the whole world: we have only to consider the United States for this fact to be vivid to us. Such effects are due not only to the external actions of the country: for instance, to the decisions of American governments which countries to bomb or to boycott, or to which national governments or rebel movements to give military support. They are due to internal policy also: whether American firms and individuals are permitted to burn fossil fuels at the present rate will affect the extent of the ecological disaster that will engulf the planet. There is an obvious reason why politicians are indifferent to such considerations: there are no votes to be gained from them. Politicians owe their positions to their national electorates: citizens of foreign countries contribute nothing to them. The system of nation-states virtually guarantees universal national selfishness.

Mankind has not yet stumbled on a satisfactory solution to this problem. It arises from the conception of 'national sovereignty', according to which no other state or international body has the right to interfere in the 'internal affairs' of any state, that is, in how it treats those it regards as its citizens. The conception of national sovereignty is undergoing erosion. Kosovo is the obvious example; but no state dares to challenge China's occupation of Tibet, and only futile protests have been aroused by Russia's attack on Chechnya. The 'international community' dares act only against those a twentieth of its size. No mechanism has been suggested for curbing the actions of a state that harm other nations, let alone the rest of the world. Nor has anyone suggested that there should be an input from the outside world into the elections held in any country. The international order contrasts strongly with the present structure of the Catholic Church, in which bishops (St Ambrose, for example) used to be elected by the diocesan laity or clergy but are now appointed by the Pope. How are we to find a *via media* between unchecked local democracy and unchecked central absolutism?

We are here concerned only with the rights of a state to refuse or accept would-be immigrants, and its duties towards them. Some hold that it is the right of every state to control its own borders, and hence at its pleasure to admit or exclude those who wish to cross them. Others believe that there ought to be no control of immigration anywhere; that all borders should be completely open. This thesis, that borders should all be open, follows from the principle of the free market: on the same grounds that goods and capital should be able to move freely across the globe, so should people. The most celebrated exponent of the free-market ideology, Milton Friedman, to his credit draws this conclusion. (Other free-market economists have made the same case, or a modified version of it.) The many eager followers of Friedman among practical politicians wholeheartedly reject that case; many of the most fervent proponents of the free market as a purely economic principle are vehement advocates of strict immigration control. The opening of all borders was also the ideal of the first post-war British Foreign Secretary, Ernest Bevin, who expressed the hope that it would become possible to do away with passports altogether. The most radical view is that this should not be viewed as an ideal, to be achieved in unison with many countries. On this view, it is a human right to stay or go wherever one wants, as it was a legal right to enter and leave the United Kingdom throughout the nineteenth century. If that really is a human right, then no state has the right to exclude anyone: it is not a matter for negotiation between countries, but an obligation on every state that respects human rights.

In his encyclical *Pacem in Terris* Pope John XXIII came close to endorsing the principle of open borders. He wrote that every human being

> when there are just reasons in favour of it, . . . must be permitted to emigrate to other countries and take up residence there. The fact that he is a citizen of a particular state does not debar him from membership of the human family, or from citizenship of that universal society, the common, worldwide fellowship of men.

Here is the foundation of every state's duty to those who are not its citizens: they are fellow human beings. No state can claim that its duties extend only to its own citizens, any more than any head of a family can declare that he has no duties except to those who belong to his family: he has special duties towards them, but he has duties to all who can be affected by his actions, inasmuch as they and he belong to the same world-wide human family. By just the same token, the citizens of any country share with others the citizenship of the universal society of human beings, and the state which represents them therefore has moral duties towards other states and citizens of those other states. In a section on refugees, *Pacem in Terris* proclaims the rights of economic migrants, including among the personal rights of each individual the 'right to enter a country in which he hopes to be able to provide more fittingly for himself and his dependants'. It continues:

> It is therefore the duty of state officials to accept such immigrants and – so far as the good of their own community, rightly understood, permits – to further the aims of those who may wish to integrate themselves into a new society.

The qualification about the good of the officials' own community is not said to restrict their duty to admit such immigrants, but only how much they are obliged to help them to integrate.

The right of states to refuse entry to whom they will cannot be absolute, since their responsibilities to the persecuted require them to admit refugees who have established their claim to asylum, at least if they cannot find any other country willing to offer them refuge. Moreover, if it is genuinely the absolute right of every person to leave his native country, some states must between them have the duty to admit those who do so. On the other hand, if a people has a right not to be submerged, each country must possess a residual right to restrict entry to it. It is true that the danger of being submerged is very rare: in modern times the only peoples to be threatened by it have been those ruled by colonial governments and by states that have illegally annexed their territories: the peoples of the Baltic states, of Tibet and of East Timor, annexed by states whose populations were strongly differentiated from their own. It is very unlikely that, without the use of such power, the people of any present-day state will run the slightest risk of being submerged by ordinary processes of immigration not specifically designed to produce that effect. That is why the right of a state to restrict immigration entailed by the right of its people not to be submerged is no more than a residual one: but it exists and therefore contradicts the claim that no right to exclude would-be entrants ever exists.

But may not that right be more than residual? Nations in danger of being submerged are always small ones in the neighbourhood of large ones. It is true that submergence has threatened only those ruled by imperial powers or annexed by expansionist ones. The colonial governments, indifferent to the desires of the people of the colonies, have encouraged immigration for economic reasons, as the British did in Malaya and Fiji; the annexing power has encouraged its people to move into the annexed territories in order to make their populations more uniform with that of the general domain, and, in many cases, precisely in order to weaken or obliterate the local culture, as the Soviet Union did in the Baltic states, as Indonesia did in East Timor and as China is doing in Tibet. But, in a world devoid of immigration controls and in which the principle of the free movement of people was generally accepted, might not something similar have happened without annexation or colonial rule? Might not Chinese have been attracted in large numbers to Malaya for economic motives, and Indians to Fiji, without official encouragement? Might not the Soviet government have encouraged emigration to the Baltic states, Indonesia have encouraged emigration to East Timor and China have encouraged emigration to Tibet, with an eye to eventual absorption of those territories by 'voluntary' popular application from within them? Such possibilities cannot be ruled out. The conclusion is that small countries have a better right to control immigration than large ones, weak countries than powerful ones.

The conclusion may be generalised. Any country has the right to limit immigration if its indigenous population is in serious danger of being rapidly overwhelmed. The word 'rapidly' is essential here. A gradual influx of people of a distinct culture is little threat to the native culture, since the immigrants will in large part assimilate the manners of their new home. They will not wholly assimilate the indigenous culture, but will contribute new elements to it. That is almost always an invigorating effect, however. The new cultural elements will be generally adopted if they are found to be compatible; it is they that will be assimilated. If they are not found to be capable of assimilation into the national culture, they will remain proper to a minority, which will be no threat to the life of the majority. In no case will a *gradual* influx of people of a distinct culture threaten a native culture, even if, over the very long run, the influx amounts to quite large numbers. The danger of submergence occurs only when the immigrants arrive in a short time in such large numbers that they see no need to assimilate.

The right of states to restrict immigration when there is a genuine danger of submergence needs to be stated, since it is not merely a theoretical possibility but is of practical relevance in certain parts of the world. It is dangerous to enunciate it, since it is liable to be seized on by the fanatics for exclusionist immigration policies who abound in present-day Europe.

They already loudly proclaim the need to resist being 'swamped', and represent an immigrant total of 5 per cent or even 2 per cent of the population as capable of swamping the native 95 per cent or 98 per cent of the remainder. It is therefore necessary, whenever this topic is discussed, to emphasise the absurdity of such misrepresentations and the rarity of a genuine danger of submergence. Yet the imminent danger that a truth will be distorted is not a ground for declining to state it.

Is the methodology of our discussion so far defective? We have been discussing one legitimate ground that a state may have for restricting immigration. We may find others: but is this the right way to examine the question? It presumes that the onus of proof lies with any claim to have a right to exclude would-be immigrants. The upshot of a discussion conducted on these lines will then be that each state ought to admit those who seek to enter its territory unless one of the exceptional circumstances that would justify a refusal applies. The conclusion would be quite different if we started with the presumption that each state had the right to refuse entry, and then set about listing special circumstances in which that right was void. Which should the preliminary presumption be? Does everyone have a presumptive right to go where he will, if he can find the means, a right that can properly be curtailed in particular circumstances? Or does no one have a right to go and to stay in any country of which he is not a citizen? May this be done only by grace of the liberality of that country?

The ascription to someone, or to everyone, of a right to do something or to have something admits of interpretations of varying strength. In its weakest sense, it means that a person (or the particular person) does no wrong by doing or having that thing, and can therefore only wrongfully be prevented or hindered from doing it or having it. In this sense I have a right to learn Quechua, and no one has a right to stop me. But this can hardly be called an inviolable right. It is difficult to think of circumstances which would prompt a European government to prohibit the learning of Quechua, let alone justify it in doing so; but were such circumstances to arise, the law could scarcely be said to be oppressive, save to a very few who had an urgent personal need to know the language. No doubt in Peru such a law would be oppressive. It is, however, an inviolable right to speak one's mother tongue. To do so is so integral a part of each individual's personality that any general interference with the use of anyone's native language, by schoolmasters, agencies of government or other authorities, must count as an infringement of an inviolable right; this obviously does not apply to rules governing what languages may be used in official assemblies or the like. Grave ethical problems can arise even about rights that are inviolable in this sense. In Western countries most people would regard it as the inviolable right of couples – at least of couples permanently bound to one another – to have children if they mutually wish, and to have as many as they wish. Is this right universal, or does it apply only to those not deemed unfit to have children by some authority? If it is universal, it is violated by laws, such as were once in force in some American states, ordaining compulsory sterilisation. Does this right include the couple's recourse to the exceptional methods medical science now offers them – artificial insemination and *in vitro* fertilisation? Could a law forbidding such means, or denying parental rights over offspring so engendered, be deemed a violation of rights? More pressingly, is the Chinese law restricting each couple to a single child a violation of human rights? In every case, a curb by the state on the exercise of a right in this sense requires urgent reason to justify it: does the Chinese government have a sufficiently urgent reason?

The rights just discussed, even if inviolable, are conditional rights: rights to do such-and-such a thing if one wishes and if one can. A Samoan resident in, say, Denmark has a right to speak Samoan if an opportunity presents itself: if there are no speakers of Samoan within striking distance, his right is not violated, but simply incapable of being exercised. If a neighbour knows of another Samoan speaker, and introduces them, that is a kindness, not an action anyone was obliged to perform. There is a stronger sense in which someone may be said to have a right: the sense in which everyone who can, and the state or subordinate authority particularly, has an obligation to secure to that person what he has a right to. It is in this absolute sense that we speak of the right to life, to sustenance and to shelter, this last far from being assured to many in almost all countries of the world.

When is a right genuinely inviolable? Certainly the rights to the minimum necessities for a human existence – food, shelter, the means for a livelihood – are inviolable; so are rights to forms of action integral to someone's living as the person he is, such as the right to the practice of one's religion, to the use of one's own language and to the temperate expression of one's opinion. Rights of the latter kind cover only those features that are personal to everyone. If a man who has been devoted to cockfighting goes to a country where it is illegal, his rights are not violated, even though he protests that cockfighting has become integral to his sense of his identity: he had no business to make it so. Against the state, rights of the former kind – rights to the essentials of a human life – are absolute, those of the latter only conditional. I may have the right to attend Mass if I wish, but the state has no duty to ensure that there is a priest to celebrate it; nor can it be required to guarantee each individual a platform from which he may proclaim his views. It does have a duty to ensure, by the electoral system or otherwise, the due representation of minorities, including racial and religious minorities, save those of negligible size; the long period when the British House of Commons was wholly white in racial composition disgraced British democracy. Significant groups of people must be assured of a means to voice their distinctive needs and perceptions; no individual can lay claim to a right to do so. The distinction between absolute and conditional rights often goes unnoticed in discussions of the 'right to free speech'; students who decline to invite speakers with racist views have been denounced as enemies of free speech, although they were not trying to prevent any such person from expressing his beliefs, but only refraining from offering him a means of propagating them. It remains that it is often a delicate matter to decide which rights are inviolable. Everyone would agree that it is every couple's right to have a child if they can, at least in the normal way, and most people outside China would think it was their inviolable right to have more than one if they wished: but there is room for dispute whether, in all circumstances, they have a right to have as many as they choose.

If there is a right to enter a country of which one is not a citizen, it is obviously in general a right only in the weaker, conditional sense. Only in special cases, such as for those fleeing persecution or banished from their native lands, can it be a right which anyone has an obligation to allow one to exercise: only those who have a means of getting to a country can exercise their right to enter it, if they have any such right. In any consideration of what we have a right to do in this conditional sense, the presumption must always be in favour of freedom. There are many things we have no right to do: but a ground must always be given for denying anyone a right to do something. No positive ground need ever be given for claiming a conditional right to do something or ascribing a conditional right to do it to someone else: the only argument that can be required is a rebuttal of a purported reason for denying that right. It is not so with the rights of a state; the presumption is never that it has a right to do whatever it likes. The rights of a state are rights over individuals, those who are its citizens and those who are not; the rights of a state towards other states are particular cases of its rights towards those who are not its citizens. The presumption for individuals is always in favour of freedom: there must be a particular ground why any state is entitled to curtail that freedom, if indeed it is. So the right of a state to refuse entry to anyone wishing to enter its territory must always be grounded in a specific reason. The onus of proof always lies with a claim to a right to exclude would-be immigrants. That is the justification of the methodology here pursued. We are not asking what specific reasons entitle someone, not a refugee, to enter the territory of a state of which he or she is not a citizen: we are asking what specific reasons may entitle a state to refuse entry to its territory. We have therefore to examine the possible bases for claiming the right to refuse entry.

4

GROUNDS OF REFUSAL

The principal actual motivation for exclusionist immigration policies is, of course, racial prejudice, or sometimes more general prejudice against foreigners, which, when present, is always felt more intensely against those who are of or are thought to be of, a different race. This has manifestly been the motive underlying all British immigration laws, and, in the past, explicitly that of American and Australian immigration laws, though happily both countries have changed in this regard; with more disguise, save among political parties of the far right, it is the principal motivation for the general agreement within the European Union that the Union's borders must be strengthened against immigrants. The desire to preserve the racial purity of the indigenous population is emphatically *not* a valid ground for excluding a particular class of immigrants or immigrants in general.

To begin with, the aim can be pursued without social disruption only if the restrictions are applied totally and before

DOI: 10.4324/9781032641683-5

the feared immigration begins. Otherwise there will already be in the country concerned a minority of people belonging to the racial group or groups despised or detested; if measures explicitly or implicitly intended to prevent the entry of members of those groups are adopted, this will inflame prejudice against those already present and foster discrimination against them. The minority will resent the laws, be indignant at the discrimination and be alienated by the racial prejudice: the social fabric will be rent and much injustice will be done. Very few restrictive immigration laws are preventive, however. Most have responded to racist or xenophobic clamour prompted by the entry of a small number of members of the racial or national group objected to. This is even true of the White Australia policy; there were Chinese miners in Australia in the second half of the nineteenth century, although no Chinese was naturalised between 1903 and 1956.

Even if the exclusionist arrangements have been put in place before any of those to be excluded have succeeded in arriving, however, the imposition of barriers plainly, let alone expressly, intended to prevent the entry of a particular race or nationality, or set of races or nationalities, is a deeply unwise policy. It will earn for the nation imposing the barriers enemies throughout the world; that nation will lose the respect of others by having chosen to brand itself illiberal and choked with racial pride. It may even inspire a bitter sense of injustice in other nations which would have liked many of their people to emigrate, as the White Australia policy did in Japan, a country suffering from gross pressure of overpopulation. (That Japan then tried to relieve this pressure by its iniquitous war with China, which was the real start of the Second World War, in no way absolves the Australian policy of being intolerably unjust.) Moreover, a racist immigration policy, like all actions inspired by racism, is intrinsically shameful, which is why it is seldom openly avowed.

Through painful experience we have learned to see race as all that it ever was, a differential distribution of a handful of minor physical characteristics, aesthetically interesting in the way that all physical characteristics can be, but having no reason to bear on how human beings should act towards one another. We have, fortunately, come a very long way in our attitudes from those nineteenth-century physical anthropologists who, in the name of science, placed Europeans on the topmost rung of the evolutionary ladder and relegated Africans to a lower rung much closer to the apes. We have come to understand that racial prejudice and the belief in one's own racial superiority are demeaning attitudes, unworthy of rational human beings as well as productive of much suffering and injustice. It cannot be admitted that any state has a right to refuse entry to intending immigrants because of their race, any more than an employer has a right to refuse applicants for jobs for that reason.

The entry of people of a different race from the indigenous majority does not threaten that majority with being submerged: submergence has to do with culture, modes of behaviour, a sense of belonging together: social factors, not physical ones. For one thing, unless the number of immigrants is massive, it is unlikely to make any perceptible difference in the long run: it has often been remarked that the considerable number of Africans living in eighteenth-century England has left no discernible effect upon the appearance of present-day English people. For another, it does not matter if it does have any such long-term effect. If it were discovered that English people of the twelfth century were notably darker in complexion than those of the present time, we should not think that they were not truly English, or that being English was not what we had thought. Still less should we think that English people of the present day were really 'coloured'. Many years ago, at about the time when racism was beginning to make itself apparent in

Britain, a British film called *Sapphire* went the rounds of the cinemas. The murder victim was a girl as white in appearance as all her friends, but a policeman, discovering her to have been the issue of a mixed marriage, stalked through the film asking all he interviewed, 'Did you know she was coloured?' – the equivalent of asking, 'Did you know she was a Jewess?' of someone discovered to have had a Jewish grandmother. We have outgrown such childish attitudes: we know that what colour you are depends on what colour you look.

Whatever the principles governing immigration policy should be, a first requirement for it to be just is that it should not be racially discriminatory. It is certainly possible to maintain immigration control without discriminating against applicants because of their race: Canada and Australia now achieve this. It is certainly more straightforward to shun direct discrimination – the use of explicitly racial criteria for admission or those intentionally designed to favour people of a certain race or races over others – than to avoid the indirect variety: indirect discrimination occurs, of course, when the criteria employed in practice favour people of a particular race although they were not devised for that end. This is very hard to avoid doing, if there is to be a system under which significantly fewer will be admitted than apply to enter. Probably the only fair way of administering such a system is to allocate points. Points will naturally be awarded to an applicant for being able to speak one of the languages of the country, for having relatives or close acquaintances already there and the like: and these will be easier to gain for people of the same kind as the principal groups making up the indigenous population or of the same origin as minority groups already present. The only way to correct this bias is to award points for such things as coming from especially needy countries or knowing languages useful for commerce or other purposes, but known to very few existing inhabitants.

Even with care to correct imbalance, some indirect discrimination will be inevitable: the essential is that the immigration control is not carried out in a spirit of racial discrimination.

This can be achieved if the will is there; but the will must inform the entire immigration service. No British Home Secretary, however determined to implement a completely racially non-discriminatory immigration policy – if such a British Home Secretary were conceivable – could do so while retaining the existing members of the immigration service. For decades they have operated on the tacit understanding that their function was to prevent the entry of as many applicants from the Indian subcontinent, the Caribbean and Africa – in short, from non-white countries – as possible. The attitude created by this understanding of their task is of course deeply ingrained: no directions from a Minister are likely to change this. The same is probably true of most European countries, Luxembourg always excepted. A real commitment to racial justice in the theory and practice of immigration control would demand great changes in bureaucratic organisation.

Because everyone recognises that it would be shameful, race is nowadays never offered as an explicit ground for excluding would-be immigrants, even though it is often the true motive. The result is that many reasons are offered which are not the true motive. Among these may be some that might be legitimate grounds for the exclusionist policy if the facts were as they presuppose. Usually the facts are not so. We are in the same position as with the danger of submergence: if we acknowledge that the grounds offered would be valid if the facts were as they presuppose, we run the risk of appearing to legitimise dishonest propaganda. Nevertheless we must consider these reasons with whatever force they would have when the facts were as claimed.

A good example is density of population. This works in the opposite direction to the danger of submergence. Evidently the inhabitants of a heavily populated country are in far less danger of being submerged by incomers differing from them culturally than those of a thinly populated country; but it may well be held that a heavily populated country has a right to exclude people applying for entry simply in order to avoid overpopulation. This plea was endlessly reiterated by opponents of immigration – i.e. Afro-Caribbean and south Asian immigration – during the many years when this was a salient political issue in Britain; everyone who ever discussed it with such opponents must have become wearied by the repetition of the phrase 'this overcrowded little island'. It is true that the population density of the United Kingdom, at 241.55 persons per square kilometre, is higher than that of Germany (227.86/sq. km.) and much higher than that of France (106.45/sq. km.), though lower than that of Belgium (330.88/sq. km.) and much lower than that of the Netherlands (453.31/sq. km.). But that those who so incessantly parroted the slogan about 'this overcrowded little island' were in truth indifferent to demographic facts as such is shown by their unawareness that, during the whole period from 1945 to 1977, there was net annual emigration from the UK: fewer people were entering the country than were leaving it. They used the argument about overcrowding solely to disguise their real concerns, which were racial, but which they knew it would have been shameful to voice.

That an argument can be dishonestly used to conceal a real motive does not show that it lacks validity. Rather the opposite; the concealment is better achieved by a valid argument, even if based on false premises, than by an invalid one. It cannot be denied that a seriously overpopulated country has the right to keep immigration below the level that would significantly exacerbate the overcrowding. In applying this principle, the effects of immigration must be viewed dispassionately. Germany has nearly as high a population density as the UK, but many more asylum seekers; the massive immigration into West

Germany after 1945 certainly contributed to the German economic miracle. The economic advantages of immigration are very marked; the density of population must be far higher than that of the UK to justify refusal of entry on that ground.

The demographic effects of immigration are generally benign. Western countries have begun to worry about the aging of their populations: as people live longer and birth rates fall, the proportion of people no longer of working age rises. The UN has estimated that Italy needs to take in about 300,000 foreign workers to replenish its aging labour force – nearly five times the number that the government has announced that it will admit from outside the EU. In a similar way, the Labour government under Harold Wilson clamped down on Commonwealth immigration in 1965 at the very time at which its Minister in charge of economic affairs was stating that Britain had a severe labour shortage. Immigrants tend in the first instance to be men and women of working age: they help to correct the skew, and they contribute proportionately more to productivity than the native inhabitants. Immigration controls work against this effect. The immigrants to Britain from both parts of Pakistan, as it then was, mostly believed that their stay would be a short one: when they had earned enough to take back to their families, they would return. They changed their minds. For one thing, the rules banned the re-entry of a settled immigrant after he had been absent to visit his family for more than two years; the danger that he would on some pretext be refused admission by a hostile immigration service even if he returned within the time limit was not negligible. The effect of this was reinforced by harsh restrictions, still in place, upon those from the 'New Commonwealth' wishing to make brief visits; in 1997 over 30 per cent of would-be visitors from Ghana were refused, compared to 0.18 per cent from Australia. The two factors combined to persuade most immigrants from

Pakistan that it was safer to stay, and send for their wives, children and aged parents to join them. The attempt to keep people out often has the effect of keeping them in; more exactly, keeping some out keeps others in. The intense efforts of the immigration service to refuse as many dependants as possible by declining to be satisfied that they were 'related as claimed' did not undo this effect, although it indeed caused a great deal of misery and separated some families for good.

The EU Office of Statistics recently published its estimates for 1999. It calculates that, but for net immigration, Germany, Italy and Sweden would all have experienced a drop in population in 1999. A UN report entitled *Replacement Migration: a Solution to Declining and Aging Populations* was published at the same time. It calculates that in Britain, Germany, Italy and France, the ratio of people of working age to those retired is now just above 4:1, but that, on present trends, it will be only 2:1 by 2050. One author of the report, J. A. Grinblat, observes that the social security systems of these countries were founded on the assumption of a 5:1 ratio. This decline, the report argues, will make it progressively harder, and eventually impossible, to provide the benefits and care needed by the elderly. It sees as the only feasible solution a great increase in the numbers of immigrants admitted; the only other possibility would be a marked raise in the age of retirement. The report's estimate of the need is substantial: an average of 5,300,000 immigrant workers per year entering the EU over the next 30 years. But the authors of the report recognise the obstacle to this solution, namely that the electorates of European countries have set their faces against the entry of immigrants and of refugees, and so against the only possible solution to the problem. Hostility to immigrants and refugees, to which the politicians have capitulated and which they have vigorously helped to foster, threatens the welfare of the increasingly elderly native populations.

Admittedly, demographic trends can by no means always be reliably extrapolated; nevertheless, the continued aging of the population of Western countries seems a safe prediction. It should not be thought that either immigrants or refugees consist largely of unskilled manual workers, though that is what they are often forced to become when they can get work at all. While the system of B vouchers for Commonwealth immigrants possessing certain skills in short supply, introduced in 1965, was in operation, it became notorious that teachers and other professionals admitted with such vouchers were frequently to be found working as bus conductors. A British Home Office report published in 1995 stated that one in three among those accepted as genuine refugees had a university first or post-graduate degree or a professional qualification; 'there were academics, senior civil servants, doctors, accountants, teachers, lawyers, engineers, business people, managers, members of the armed forces, office workers, nurses, technicians, mechanics, drivers, electricians, shop assistants, factory workers, security guards and waiters'. Only 5 per cent were unskilled. If they are not blocked by racial or xenophobic discrimination from doing jobs for which they are qualified, the entry both of refugees and of immigrants is likely to be of great benefit to the economy of the country that admits them.

Many other arguments are used by advocates of tight immigration controls. There seems little reason to consider them all in detail, since all are fallacious: they are expressions of racist attitudes or general hostility to foreigners rather than the product of serious assessment. Immigrants are regularly said to be a drain on the welfare services; since the first arrivals are of working age and sometimes come from a culture which deters them from seeking assistance from outsiders, as being shameful, it is obvious that they tend to take less from those services than do the natives. It is immigration control that is a drain on the resources of the state; it costs scores of millions a year in Britain. It is also said that immigrants cause unemployment. There is no evidence for this whatever. On the contrary, it is well known that immigrants frequently take jobs which indigenous workers are reluctant to take, even when there is no alternative, because they are unpleasant, dirty, dangerous or low-paid. In times of high unemployment, the immigrants take such jobs because they are the only ones available and they are ready to do them; when there is great discrimination against them, they are the only jobs that they are not refused. The accusation is merely part of the standard litany of complaints against foreigners, made in every country for a certain time after a new batch of people arrives from elsewhere, unless they are manifestly wealthy: they are dirty, they are noisy, they steal, they will not work but just want to live on welfare, they fill up the hospitals, they crowd out the schools, they will not adopt our ways, they live in overcrowded houses, they run down the neighbourhood, the Government does more for them than it does for us. If they are wealthy, a new set of stock complaints is made: they are buying everything up, they make prices rise, they look down on us, they think they're too good for us, they've got the ear of the Government. These are not observations of reality: simply expressions of unthinking resentment.

The ground for curtailing immigration that has the least merit of all is that encapsulated in the slogan, endlessly repeated by British politicians, 'firm but fair immigration control is the key to good race relations'. The principle is the same as that on which the Australian government refused to take refugees from Hitler on the ground that they would create a 'Jewish problem'. We shall see that in Britain the continual tightening of immigration restrictions was not only a futile attempt to appease racism, but served to justify and inflame it.

Among European nations there is widespread agreement that the way to reduce immigration pressure is to give aid to the poor countries from which the immigrants come. The disparity between rich and poor nations has indeed become a scandal that must no longer be allowed to disfigure the world order. According to the *Financial Times*, the ratio of real income per head in the richest countries to that in the poorest, which was three to one at the start of the nineteenth century and 10:1 in 1900, has risen by 2000 to 60:1. At present no serious attempt is being made to redress this gross disparity: it is of the utmost urgency, and an imperative demand of justice, that the wealthy nations of the West and their agencies – the International Monetary Fund (IMF), the World Bank – should act in concert to redress this grotesque inequity. Until it is redressed, the flow of immigrants from poor countries to the rich First World will continue: if they are prevented from getting in legally, they will get in illegally. Without doubt the correction of this terrible imbalance would greatly reduce the flow of people from the poor countries to the wealthy ones.

Yet, until the condition of the impoverished countries has been improved, justice also requires that the rich countries should not shut their doors against the poor. The panic determination, extending as high as Romano Prodi, to prevent immigration to the countries of the European Union, is hysterical and profoundly unjust. At present, European nations, while piously protesting their disapproval of racism and xenophobia, in practice behave like a Dives whose response to the sight of Lazarus at his gates is to strengthen the locks. It is unlikely that the entry of immigrants from poor countries will adversely affect the economies of the wealthier countries. It will certainly assist those of the countries from which they come by the remittances they will send to their families at home. But even if it were slightly to enrich the sending countries at the cost of slightly reducing the wealth of the receiving ones – which there is no reason for supposing that it would – it would remain a foul injustice for Western nations to continue to say to them 'Keep out! Starve if you have to, but do not threaten our prosperity'.

The amelioration of the economic condition of a poor country will in the long run reduce emigration from it. It may not do so in the short term, however. In the short term, the effect of the first stage in the process of lifting the country out of the depths of poverty may be to enable people who previously could not afford to emigrate to save up enough to pay the fare: the first result of a serious attempt to relieve that country's destitution may be to increase, not decrease, the number of those who leave it for more prosperous lands. This is no argument for not doing whatever is needed to bring the poor countries of the world out of their present condition of misery: only a warning against the illusion that the first few steps in such a process constitute the solution to 'the problem of immigration'. As long as the immense contrast between rich nations and poor ones persists, justice, which requires the wealthy to correct it as rapidly and as completely as they can, also demands that the wealthy nations should not raise and strengthen their barriers against the entry of people from the poor ones.

With Britain in the lead, the nations of the European Union have adopted three tactics for keeping the numbers of immigrants and of refugees to a minimum. The rules for admitting the one and granting asylum to the other are made very restrictive. It must be made very difficult even to reach the frontiers of those countries to ask for admission or to claim asylum. This is done by imposing visa requirements on all the countries from which immigrants or refugees are likely to come, and heavy fines upon carrying companies and even lorry drivers for bringing those without 'proper papers'. That this practice, as a means of preventing refugees from reaching a place of safety, is an iniquity was already stated in the preceding chapter. It is also wrong as a means of preventing those hoping to be admitted as immigrants from having the chance to make the request: to the extent that it is unjust to refuse would-be immigrants, it must also be unjust to erect obstacles to their ever asking to be admitted, and certainly to stigmatise them as criminals when they avail themselves of the only means of entry not yet closed to them. The third tactic is the creation of disincentives, in the form of detention centres, forcible dispersal and the reduction of welfare benefits. This, too, was discussed in the previous chapter: so far, it has been used only against asylum seekers. All these measures swell the numbers of those who enter illegally.

One of the greatest social evils from which the countries of the West now suffer – those of North America as well as European ones – is the presence of illegal immigrants. This is not an evil because those people are there, in those countries: it is an evil because they are illegally there. Being in the country illegally, they are denied the rights to social security, to health care, to work and so on, that everyone ought to have and that it is the will of the state that everyone should have; and they are also at the mercy of exploiters, who pay them derisory wages or drive them into prostitution by threatening to reveal their illegal presence to the authorities. They are illegally in the country because they found their conditions at home intolerable, and yet the barriers erected with the intention of keeping them out by the country to which they have fled were too high for them to surmount by regular means. The erection of those barriers frequently fails to fulfil its intended purpose; but it has calamitous unintended consequences. The solution is not to build them higher yet: it is to lower them or, better, to dismantle them altogether.

We have seen that it is the duty of each state not merely to accept refugees, but to help them when they arrive to settle into the country that has given them refuge. The same applies, though in less urgent degree, to immigrants newly arrived. Refugees arrive bewildered, traumatised, nervous and confused: immigrants usually arrive in a good condition, and hence with a great deal less need of help. They nevertheless often do need help. A state will do well to take some pains to induct them into their new country: to provide reception centres where they can live temporarily until they find their own accommodation; to lay on language teaching for those who need it, together with explanations of legal rights and duties, how to obtain advice or legal and medical assistance, and, in general, how to manage in society. Canada and Australia do offer such basic first assistance. To do so need cost little; it will not only give an impression of welcome, but save a great deal of pointless trouble later.

In the rare cases in which it can be foreseen that the conditions from which refugees have escaped will come to a rapid end, it is of course legitimate for states to offer temporary refuge. When the Albanian-speaking residents of Kosovo were brutally forced out of their homeland, the neighbouring countries perforce took them in, but could not accommodate them for any extended period. Western governments quite rightly gave them temporary refuge, correctly expecting that the strange war against Serbia would bring their persecution to an end. Now the British Home Office is pressing them hard to return, on the ground that there is no more persecution. This pressure is legalistic. Kosovo is not yet in a condition to cope with the return of many more of its former inhabitants. Temporary asylum should last, not merely until the conditions for granting it have ceased, but until the homeland of the refugees is ready to receive them back.

From our discussion it follows that national statesmen should cease to say on behalf of the states for which they speak, 'Ours is a sovereign nation which has, in virtue of its sovereignty, the right to decide who may enter our country and who may not'. Instead, they ought to say, 'We represent our nation among the community of nations, and therefore have no right to erect barriers against people of other countries wishing to enter ours'. The idea that national frontiers should everywhere be open should become far more than a remote aspiration: it should become a principle recognised by all as the norm. We have repudiated the extreme view that this principle is absolute, with its corollary that it is one of the human rights of each individual to go wherever in the world he chooses and can afford to go. We have repudiated it by allowing that in two rare cases a state does have the right to exclude intending immigrants: that in which its people are in genuine danger of being submerged; and that in which the number wishing to enter would bring about serious overpopulation. For Western nations, however, neither threat is at all likely to occur in any foreseeable future; and we have recognised no other grounds which entitle a state to bar prospective immigrants from entering. It follows that, as things now stand, the principle of open frontiers ought to be accepted as the norm: a norm from which deviation can be justified only in quite exceptional circumstances.

Is this conclusion a mere consequence of the methodology we adopted, placing the burden of proof, not on the immigrant's case for entry, but on the state's decision to refuse entry? It would be no great criticism if it could be shown to be, since, as previously argued, it is the right methodology. The suggestion is, however, a half-truth. If we had adopted the opposite methodology, we should indeed never have arrived at the principle of open frontiers as an ideal, let alone a norm. We should have drawn up a list of circumstances in which a would-be immigrant ought, other things being equal, to be admitted. The list would have begun with the requirement of family unity. The desire to join what one has always regarded as one's family, whether by birth or adoption, and the desire to be reunited with members of one's family, are indeed compelling claims, which all states ought to respect. The list would include, below this, many other factors, such as the possession by one who finds it hard to obtain employment in his country of origin of a skill needed by the country to which he wants to immigrate. Until immigration policy is generally liberalised, it is very useful to draw up such a list, because the decisions of immigration officials would become much fairer if they were required to admit people satisfying such objective criteria: at present, those of most countries make highly subjective decisions, being given by law a great width of discretion. But, however humane and generous the list, it would be bound to leave without a valid claim on any score it included a great many people who would have prospered in the country they wished to enter and have made a signal contribution to it. And it would never become so comprehensive as to suggest the exclusion of hardly anyone but terrorists and criminals. Adoption of the methodology that places the burden of proof on intending immigrants would have made it impossible to endorse the principle of open frontiers as a general norm. It does not follow that the correct methodology, placing the burden of proof on refusals by the state, already contained the principle of open frontiers in embryo. Others, following the same methodology, might have arrived at a different conclusion, reckoning several other circumstances as entitling a state to bar its frontiers to would-be immigrants. They would, in my view, be wrong to do so, but not because they had been asking the wrong questions. The correct methodology does not of itself entail the principle of open frontiers.

The acceptance of that principle by Western states requires a complete transformation of current Western attitudes to immigration. Its politicians preach the need for the most rigid controls; its peoples have been subjected to such preaching for decades. The urgent need is for the leaders of the nation of the West to make a volte-face – what is commonly called a U-turn – and start explaining the necessity for a wholly new relation between the prosperous nations of the world and the poorer ones. That is impossible, it may be objected. No country's populace is inclined to listen to moral exhortation to put up with what it is not disposed to have, for the sake of the people of other countries, still less to consider abstract questions of political philosophy. But the fact is that the issue is not just one of theory or of moral principle: it is of pressing practical import. The present world order is already grossly inefficient, calling upon the rich nations to pay out to relieve famines and other sudden disasters such as floods caused by the stripping of forested regions and the destruction by earthquakes of houses which could not be built safely because of the cost. Of course, the relief is seldom nearly enough, and not maintained for nearly long enough; it is due to our mismanagement of the world that it needs to be given at all as often as it does. The horrifying inequity of the world order cannot endure indefinitely: sooner or later it will produce an explosion that will have catastrophic effects upon the countries of the First World. Already the immigration system in many countries is collapsing under the pressure of demand: a backlog of asylum claims builds up; the immigration service makes ridiculous mistakes which cause justified indignation; rounding up overstayers by brutal means they take innocent lives, such as Joy Gardner's; a great underclass of illegal immigrants frays the edges of social order. It is stupidity, as well as injustice, to continue as we are doing: the public of every Western country must be made aware of this.

A volte-face is not impossible. In the 1970s both Canada and Australia completely reversed their hitherto flagrantly racist immigration policies and adopted non-racial ones. This is possible only in two circumstances: if the public has been educated to change its attitudes, or else the attitudes of the public have spontaneously changed, and it demands a matching change in government policies. It is doubtless possible for

European governments to begin the process of re-educating their electorates – there are few signs of a spontaneous change of heart. Since all those governments are committed in theory to the eradication of racial discrimination, they can easily announce that they propose to eradicate it from the operation of the immigration service: it would be hard for anyone to object. A total volte-face from one day to the next by the endorsement of the principle of open borders as an ideal is doubtless impracticable. But governments can denounce the disgusting propaganda against refugees now being spewed out by the popular press, instead of abetting it, as they now do, by speeches castigating 'bogus asylum seekers and criminal elements'; they can repudiate it as untruthful and racially inflammatory. They can also commence the task of conveying to their publics that the maintenance of pensions for the retired above the poverty level will demand the entry of foreign workers on a large scale. Once a realisation of this fact has softened the public mind, attitudes to immigration and to refugees will automatically start to change: and governments will be able, at the same time as re-educating their publics, to alter their policies on both. They can, first, start to apply decent criteria for assessing asylum claims, and even exercise a little compassion in the process. They can lower the barriers to ordinary immigration, and adopt a system such as Canada has operated for many years now. Under the Canadian system, refugees and family dependants have first priority: after them, the rest are judged on a points system. Along with all this, European governments can dismantle the devices they have been using to prevent refugees from ever reaching their countries – visa requirements and fines on carriers; and they can stop punitive treatment of refugees when they have arrived – detention, forced dispersal, denial of social security, vouchers instead of cash. The litmus test will be the treatment of Gypsies. It always has been: for centuries, ever since they reached Europe, the Gypsies have been the most heartlessly persecuted minority in the continent, persecuted even more severely than the Jews. The land in which Gypsies seeking refuge are able to find it and to be treated with kindness by its authorities will be one in which justice flourishes. With such policies pursued, and governments appealing simultaneously to self-interest and a sense of compassion and of fairness among their peoples, the whole atmosphere will gradually change.

Such a change will be possible only if the amelioration of immigration and asylum policies is accompanied by a determined effort to eradicate racism and its sibling, xenophobia. This evil pair, in their manifold forms, are the roots from which most human evils stem, hatred of immigrants and refugees among them. That effort must attack, not only expressions of hatred and contempt, but every form of practical discrimination. Those attitudes, with the practices that spring from them, are highly sensitive to the prevailing social climate, a climate much influenced by the manifest behaviour of politicians and others prominent in a society. If they have the courage, not just for mild deprecation of bigotry, but to voice their contempt for it, and to display by their actions that they are uninfected by it, they can contribute to altering the social climate. Some progress over the last fifteen years can be observed in Britain, although there remain knots of intense committed racists, and the attitudes of politicians have regressed a long way. Good progress has also been made in some European countries such as the Netherlands; in others little has yet been achieved in this regard. Only when racism and xenophobia come to be overwhelmingly despised will change come about in the administration of immigration policy. When it does, then, eventually, the principle of open borders will be able to be set up as the ideal to be attained, with proper acknowledgement of the right of states under special threat to refuse entry.

5

CITIZENSHIP

In most countries, citizenship is a status defined in a constitution; it carries with it certain civil rights, in particular the right to vote. In Britain the position is quite different. Historically, Britain has operated with the concept, not of citizenship, but of subjecthood, a feudal link between monarch and individual, each side having duties towards the other. Never having abolished the monarchy or produced a modern written constitution, and never adopting a theory of the state in which rights derive from membership of that state, Britain has a unique and uneasy concept of citizenship. Historically, it was the status of British subject, not that of citizen of the UK, that conferred civil rights – the right to vote, to serve on juries, to work in the civil service. The ghost of this conception survives under the British Nationality Act of 1981, it being citizenship of some Commonwealth country that confers the right to vote and the rest. The British concept of citizenship is defined by ordinary statute law. It is entangled

DOI: 10.4324/9781032641683-6

with the old subject status and with immigration status in ways which only an expert can disentangle.

The modern concept of a citizen is proper to republics. Citizens collectively participate in the political process: those who govern do so in accordance with the will of the people, that is, of the citizens at large. They are responsible to the citizens, and may be removed by them if they fail to implement the will of the people. They are not the subjects of authority, but free men and women who are the source of authority.

In historical practice, of course, as absolute monarchy yielded in Britain to the constitutional variety, and the principle of democracy made its gradual headway in the political arrangements, the concept of subjecthood became divested of much of its feudal character; but it still amounted to little more than a set of entitlements held by most inhabitants of the Empire. Meanwhile, in republics, the will of the people – a stirring notion difficult to define with precision, perhaps incapable of being so defined – came to be identified with the outcome of whatever electoral system happened to be in force at any given time. But it is from the concept of citizenship that our prevailing notions of the rights and duties of a state derive. Those who continue to proclaim the sovereignty of the nation-state regard it as existing to safeguard the welfare of its citizens, and only them. It is from this conception that there stems the notion that it has an absolute right to bar from crossing its frontiers anyone it chooses to bar; as does the idea that every citizen has an absolute right to cross or reside within those frontiers. Under feudal law, it was quite different: the sovereign had an unchallengeable right to bar, invite in, banish or expel whom he wished.

It was argued in preceding chapters that states should retain the right to control entry and can legitimately exercise it in certain exceptional circumstances, but that all states ought to recognise the normal principle to be that of open borders, allowing all freely to enter and, if they will, to settle in, any country that they wish. The moral imperative that demands this was stated by Pope John XXIII in his encyclical *Pacem in Terris*, quoted in Chapter 3. In it he said that, 'when there are just reasons in favour of it', every human being 'must be permitted to emigrate to other countries and take up residence there'. The reason he gave for this was that the fact that someone is a citizen of a particular state 'does not debar him from membership of the human family, or from citizenship of that universal society, the common, worldwide fellowship of men'. As we saw, Pope John even went some way in the same encyclical towards declaring economic migration a basic human right, saying that 'among man's personal rights we must include his right to enter a country in which he hopes to be able to provide more fittingly for himself and his dependants'.

It was argued in the preceding chapters that the state has a legitimate right to impose any large-scale restriction on immigration only in quite special circumstances. It must also be accorded the right to refuse admission to individuals whose presence would be dangerous, or might reasonably be feared to be so – suspected terrorists, drug dealers and criminals. The recognition that such people may legitimately be excluded would risk refusals based on whim or prejudice if the decisions were in the hands of executive officials alone. Intending immigrants ought to be told of reasons why they are refused, and given the opportunity to appeal against the decision before a tribunal independent of the immigration service. Such tribunals should not be required simply to accept a Minister's – let alone an official's – judgement that the presence of a given individual would be undesirable: specific grounds should be offered, and tested by evidence and argument before the tribunal. Only when the ground given concerns national security should its details be withheld from the public and released only to the adjudicators.

If the principle of open borders is accepted as the norm, entry to a country and residence in it will largely cease to be one of the privileges of citizenship. What of other privileges? The most obvious of these is the right to vote. Immigrants, once resident in the country, pay rates and taxes: should they not enjoy the right to take part in the election of local and national legislatures, in accordance with the famous principle 'No taxation without representation'? All states provide for foreigners who have lived some time in the country some means of being naturalised and thus becoming citizens. The required length of residence varies greatly; in most countries acceptance of an application to be naturalised is in the discretion of a Minister, who is not required to give reasons for refusal and against whose decision there is no appeal. The conditions to be satisfied are in some countries light, in others so arduous as to be almost impossible to meet. Some, such as Germany, require the applicant to renounce his former citizenship; others allow dual nationality. But only a few (for example Sweden and the Netherlands) grant the vote to anyone who is not a citizen, and then only in local, not in national, elections.

On the face of it, a denial of the vote to non-citizens is unjust. Someone who has chosen to live in a country, contributing by his work to its prosperity and by his payment of its taxes to its government ought surely to be as entitled as anyone else to exert whatever little influence he can on who governs it and what its laws shall be. It may be argued that paying a country's taxes does not entitle one to political representation. The immigrant enjoys the protection of the country's laws: that privilege is enough to justify demanding its taxes from him. If he wanted to be able to vote, he could always have been naturalised.

There may be many reasons why he has not been naturalised, however. He may not be qualified to apply, having not lived in the country for long enough or failing to satisfy one of the other conditions imposed. He may have applied and failed the language test, examination on the constitution or whatever other qualifying procedure he underwent. He may have applied and been refused, with no reason given (this may have been due to a confusion between two individuals with the same name on some list). Above all, he may not have applied because the state does not allow dual nationality, and he wants to retain citizenship of his country of origin: he is afraid, if he has renounced its citizenship, of being refused entry when he returns to see his native land once more or to visit his relatives, or perhaps even to go back for good when a new regime is established. Yet he may have lived in the country for 3 years, or 12, or 18, obeyed its laws and been 'a good citizen' in every way that he could without being a citizen. Immigrants such as himself may have some special needs which will be overlooked if they are unrepresented, or opinions which will never gain a public hearing. Denying him the vote is surely to be deemed unjust.

It is unjust. In ideal circumstances, it would not happen. But whenever there is public hostility, or any danger of public hostility, to immigrants, it would be imprudent to give the vote to residents regardless of whether they were citizens or not. To do so would exacerbate the hostility: a scare could easily be whipped up that admitting them in any numbers would change the politics of the country: 'The immigrant vote will deny us any voice in how the country is run', the populist press will warn. This will of course be as great a nonsense as everything else the populist press says in order to stimulate hatred of immigrants; but its readers will believe it because of the pleasure they derive from being given a reason for hating one or another group of people. So to give the vote to residents at large is not practicable, although perhaps to give it just for local elections might be. Rather, what should be urged are liberal naturalisation laws. There should be a general international agreement to allow dual nationality. The period of residence required before naturalisation should never be greater than three years. If any tests are imposed, they should be easy to pass, even for the not very bright. Grounds for refusal should always be stated, and should be subject to appeal.

If aliens should normally be admitted and allowed to reside, and if, in an ideal world, they should be allowed to vote as soon as they establish residence, or if, under existing conditions, they should be speedily enabled to become citizens without any great difficulty, what difference would remain between citizens and resident aliens?

The primary duty of a state is to administer just laws and ensure just conditions for those living within its boundaries, whether citizens or aliens; and it has only limited rights to deny entry to aliens. The principal difference between the claims that members of the two categories have upon it is therefore manifest when they are not living within its boundaries. Every state has the duty to protect its citizens when, travelling in foreign lands, they find themselves under threat, and to help them when they simply get into difficulties. Every individual needs to have a government which will provide such protection and such help: that is why there ought to be no stateless persons. No state has such a duty towards individuals not its citizens and living outside its jurisdiction: only in cases of gross violations of the human rights of whole groups of people is it justified in acting to protect those who are not its own. Once within a country, anyone, whether citizen or not, puts himself under the protection of its government, and is entitled to receive it. Even the most rigorous interpretation of this principle, which would allow that no one can be fully protected by the law unless he is allowed to take part in the process of choosing the legislature, does not obliterate the distinction between those who are and those who are not citizens. Everyone, wherever he is, has the right to call on the protection and assistance of the state whose citizenship he holds.

That may be the major rationale of the institution of citizenship: but what of those citizens who need protection from their own states? We have recently seen the hesitant beginnings of intervention, on behalf of such citizens, by international agencies – normally by the United Nations, but, in the case of Kosovo, by NATO: intervention that has so far been either clumsy or inefficient and ineffective. Whether this will develop into a genuinely effective means of defending people from gross oppression the future will disclose. In the meantime, there is only one form of protection that can ordinarily be offered: the ready acceptance by other states of those of the oppressed who can contrive to escape as refugees. That is why the Old Testament so frequently enjoins charity towards three particular groups: widows, orphans and strangers. Members of all three categories are deprived of their natural protectors: they have for this reason a compelling claim upon the protection of others. A claim that ought to be recognised by all the governments of the world as compelling, but which, unhappily, so many are now resolved to resist.

Part 2

HISTORY

6

HOW IMMIGRATION
WAS MADE A MENACE
IN BRITAIN

In 1961 Britain was a profoundly racist country. Is it still, now in 2000? Well, at least not as overtly racist as in 1961. In 1961, it was commonplace for advertisements for accommodation, in the press and on notices displayed on front doors, to bear the words, 'No Coloureds'; it remained commonplace until the passing in 1968 of the second Race Relations Act, which made racial discrimination in housing illegal. Only those barred by such notices, together with a small handful of white people ideologically opposed to racism and committed to the equal treatment of people of all races, were offended by them; for most white people, they were as natural and unobjectionable as notices saying 'No children or dogs'. Probably now, in 2000, the majority of British people would be shocked by such a

DOI: 10.4324/9781032641683-8

notice. They would not think merely that it was against the law: they would think it contemptible and wrong. But there certainly remain a number who would be heartened by seeing such a notice and mentally cheer the householder who put it up. When, in April 1998, around the anniversary of Enoch Powell's notorious racist speech – the so-called 'rivers of blood' speech – a television debate on the motion that Powell had inflamed racial hatred was broadcast, the motion was defeated, to loud cheers, by the votes of a solid majority of the studio audience. This was, no doubt, accounted for in part by the ineptitude of the prosecution team and possibly by the faulty wording of the motion, which included the accusation that Powell was personally a racist; it should have been obvious that, if Powell cynically exploited racist feelings that he did not share, his behaviour was even more heinous than if he spoke from the heart. All the same, it is obvious that no one could vote against a motion condemning for stirring up racist feelings a man who had said that, by admitting people with darker skins, the nation was heaping up its own funeral pyre, without being deeply imbued with such feelings, doubtless unacknowledged, of his or her own. Only the producers of the programme can tell how the studio audience was selected; but it will surprise some, and deeply discourage many, that it was possible in 1998 to assemble any large body of British people well over 50 per cent of whom were prepared to reveal their latent racism by voting to vindicate Enoch Powell.

There is plenty of evidence of enduring racism in 2000. Violent racial attacks, including murders, have increased, together with vicious racial taunting of children and adults. After many decades during which almost every member of the racial minorities have been well aware of it, the police have at last acknowledged the existence of racist attitudes and behaviour within the force. Statistics prove that racial discrimination in employment still blights the chances of many for a successful life. Nevertheless, Britain in 2000 is less openly racist than Britain in 1961, indeed than many European countries in 2000. In 1961, the employees of a bus company could go on strike if the company took on a 'coloured' conductor; bank managers could explain that they could not employ 'coloured' tellers because their customers would not like it; in any public discussion of race, someone was bound to ask, as a clincher, 'How would you feel if your daughter was to marry one?'. Such things are unthinkable now, not merely because the law prohibits discrimination in employment, but because the prevalent attitudes have changed.

It is frequently said that racial prejudice goes very deep. This is a fallacy: it is in fact extremely shallow. It is said to be deep because it is often intense and always implacably resistant to rational persuasion; but neither characteristic implies depth. *Why* would no present-day bank manager say that he could not employ 'coloured' bank tellers because his customers would not like it? The trite answer is, 'Because he knows that he would be disapproved of for saying that'. This answer, true enough, requires analysis. It is not that a bank manager would think to himself, 'That's what I'd like to say, but I'd better not, because people would disapprove of me for saying it'. Quite the contrary: *he* would be shocked if he heard that any other bank manager had said it. Even though he himself, as a very young bank manager, had said exactly that at some time in the 1960s, he would now strenuously and quite sincerely deny that he ever would or could have said such a thing.

In this matter, and doubtless in very many others, a great many people not merely conform to but internalise the attitudes it is respectable to express in the milieux they inhabit at the time; they make those attitudes their own. Because they have consistently done this all their lives, they are not conscious of having changed, and in a sense they have not changed: and so they project back into their pasts the attitudes they now have. When apartheid was in force in South Africa, white South African visitors to Britain would respond to criticism of the regime by liberal white Britons that the critics would quickly change their views if they were to come to South Africa and experience it for themselves. And in most cases they were quite right: a short time spent surrounded by white defenders of apartheid in South Africa would quickly have transformed most white British people into carbon copies of them. Experience would have taught them nothing that they had not known before: immersion in their new environment would merely have eroded their feelings for justice and equality. The converse is also true. Put the moderately racially prejudiced in surroundings in which the expression of such prejudice would not be tolerated – in a newly independent African state, for instance – and all vestige of that prejudice will rapidly evaporate from their mentality; again, they would stoutly, even contemptuously, deny that it had ever been present. Racial attitudes, whether benign or the converse, are very often shallow components of the human psyche: they can then be easily scraped off by the abrasion of a social milieu unfavourable to them. To create a social climate in which it is disreputable to evince racial hostility is the only way in which to eliminate, not merely the expression of the feeling, but the feeling itself.

To describe racist attitudes as shallow is not to call them trivial. Quite the contrary: racial hatred and illusions of racial superiority underlay the two most horrifying crimes of the second millennium AD, the Nazi Holocaust of Jews and Gypsies and the translatlantic slave trade and the New World slavery that it subserved. Wherever racism has manifested itself, it has given rise to crimes and mean unkindnesses, inflicting misery on thousands and ripping society apart.

Racist attitudes were expressed by the British ruling class as early as 1953. In December of that year a Home Office Working Party on 'Coloured People seeking Employment in the UK' was set up, to 'examine the possibilities of preventing any further increase in coloured people seeking employment in the UK'.[1] In 1961, the general British public was beginning to get worked up about the 'racial problem'. In that year, the Conservative Government announced in the Queen's speech a Bill to impose immigration controls upon Commonwealth citizens. Under the British Nationality Act of 1948, all citizens of Commonwealth countries had a dual status. They were citizens of some one country belonging to the Commonwealth, say Canada, Australia, India or Pakistan; citizens of Britain or of any of its colonies were 'citizens of the UK and Colonies'. But they also had a status superior to this citizenship and common to all: they were British subjects. It was in virtue of this overriding status that, when in Britain, they were entitled to vote and to serve on juries: it still is, although the term 'British subject' has been replaced in law by 'Commonwealth citizen'. But it was also in virtue of their status as British subjects that citizens of independent Commonwealth countries and of the colonies were entitled to enter Britain at their will, without being subject to immigration control. The newly announced Commonwealth Immigration Bill would change all that: it would impose immigration controls on Commonwealth citizens, just as aliens – citizens of foreign countries not in the Commonwealth – were subject to them.

As this legislation was to apply to citizens of independent countries in the Commonwealth such as Canada, there was some legal, and arguably some moral, colour to this, even if it dealt a blow to the whole conception of the Commonwealth. Such independent countries were entitled to maintain their own immigration laws, and these did not always guarantee the right of entry to all British subjects; in 1946 Canada had passed an Act establishing her own citizenship. But for the imposition of immigration control on citizens of British colonies there was no justification of any kind. They had the same status and the same passports as residents of Britain born in the country, with the same rhetoric about HM Secretary of State requesting and requiring: both were citizens of the UK and Colonies. The only difference was the stamp showing where the passport was issued. The legal fiction offered to justify imposing immigration controls upon them was that their passports were issued by the colonial government, and not by the British Government. But the fiction was transparent. Obviously, a colonial government cannot issue a passport on its own behalf: it has no representation in other countries, and has no way to protect its citizens when they travel abroad. A British colonial government issues passports *on behalf of* the British Government, whose agent it is.

The transparency of this fiction did not prevent Parliament from passing this Bill into law in 1962, against the strong, principled opposition of the Labour and Liberal members and of a few Conservatives. The Act was not racially discriminatory in form, applying as it did to all Commonwealth citizens; its motivation was purely racial. As Sir Alec Douglas-Home had written, when Secretary of State for Commonwealth Relations, as early as 1955:

> On the one hand it would presumably be politically impossible to legislate for a colour bar and any legislation would have to be non-discriminatory in form. On the other hand we do not wish to keep out immigrants of good type from the old Dominions. I understand that, in the view of the Home Office, immigration officers could, without giving rise to trouble or publicity, exercise such a measure of discrimination as we think desirable.[2]

The Home Office has remained of the same opinion to this day. The contrast between the old Commonwealth, immigrants from which were tacitly understood to be of good type, as shown by their colour, and the new Commonwealth, understood as sending immigrants of poor type and the wrong colour, was frequently drawn in the years from 1962 onwards.

The Conservative Government, in putting the Bill before Parliament, was actuated in part by the prejudices of its own members, but more largely by pressure from right-wing politicians such as Cyril Osborne, Lord Elton, Gerald Nabarro, Ronald Bell and Duncan Sandys, from Conservative party associations in many parts of the country and from some small right-wing but well-financed pressure groups – the Immigration Control Association, the Racial Preservation Society, the British Rights Society and the Society for Individual Freedom. From this moment on, immigration and race became inextricably entangled in the public mind. In the minds of many, they were entangled well before 1962. A letter published in the *Hull Daily Mail* in April 1955 said:

> Except for the genuine student, all further coloured immigration to this country should be halted before a colour problem is introduced into a country where one did not exist.[3]

This is comparable to the Australian government's reason for refusing Jewish refugees from Hitler: they would create a Jewish problem. In the eyes of the racist, it is the *presence* of people against whom the prejudice is directed which constitutes the problem, not the prejudice against them. This attitude became very common, and was perfectly illustrated by a Minister of the Labour Government who announced in 1966 that he was about to visit a particular city, 'where the problem is greatest'. He did not mean 'where racism is most virulent': he meant 'where there is the greatest number of black people'. And so the clamour of the increasingly vociferous racist groups in Britain was always to STOP IMMIGRATION. The term 'immigration' came by itself to mean 'coloured immigration' – the immigration of people from the Caribbean and the Indian sub-continent; it was not applied to the immigration of white people from Australia and elsewhere. It was a code-word. The people who demanded an end to immigration were not concerned with migration as such, even though they often talked of 'this crowded little island'. If they had been, they would have been relieved by the fact that, throughout the 1960s and 1970s, Britain was a country of net emigration: more people left than arrived. They would, however, have been worried by the thousands of Hungarians who came in 1956 or the thousands of Chileans who came after 1972: but they were not, for these were not 'immigrants' in the coded sense of the term.

Imposing controls on immigration from the Commonwealth was, from 1962 onwards, a very convenient means for governments to appease racist agitation. As Sir Alec Douglas-Home had remarked, it was not discriminatory in form: to accusations of racial discrimination, governments could always reply, 'The Act/regulation says nothing about colour or race: it applies to everybody'. And, as Sir Alec also indicated, a tip to the immigration officers about what was expected of them would ensure that it was discriminatory in practice. As the word 'immigration' was a code, so immigration control was a code. It said, 'We do not want these people here: we are doing everything we can to keep them out'. It was intended to mean that: it was understood as meaning that. It was unnecessary to specify why it was important to reduce 'immigration'. Everyone knew why it was important: it was better not to spell it out.

In 1964 Labour won the election, with a very small majority in the House of Commons. Some of those who voted Labour and had been shocked by the Commonwealth Immigrants Act of 1962 believed, on the basis of Labour's opposition to that Bill and of vague remarks during the election, that the new Government would repeal the Act. They experienced a sorry surprise. The election campaign of the Conservative candidate in Smethwick, Peter Griffiths, was openly racist: against the national trend, he won, defeating the sitting MP, Patrick Gordon Walker. Gordon Walker became Foreign Secretary in the incoming Government, and was allotted what was thought to be a safe Labour seat in Leyton, where a by-election was created by the elevation of the sitting member, Reg Sorensen, to the Lords. In January 1965 Gordon Walker contrived to lose again. The newspapers strove to represent this failure as the consequence of racist opposition to the Labour party. It was probably not due to this at all, but the Government panicked. It plainly concluded that the only way to hold on to votes was to pacify racist demands for immigration control; almost immediately the Home Secretary announced new measures to repatriate 'illegal immigrants' – the first mention of a category since then heard of ad nauseam – and to tighten the regulations on entry. In August 1965 the Government published a White Paper on immigration from the Commonwealth, detailing the very considerable tightening that was intended. The White Paper was a remarkable document, in that it vigorously affirmed the need for a tightening of the immigration controls, but finished with a section refuting one by one every conceivable reason for supposing that they needed tightening. It did not matter. Those who pressed for severer controls of 'immigration' did not care for what reason the Government was imposing them, or if it was doing so for no reason at all save to pacify the individuals and groups exerting the pressure: all that concerned them was that they had found that, with the aid of the Press, they could get their way.

To conciliate those supporters who were dismayed by the volte-face, the Government introduced the first Race Relations Act to outlaw certain very restricted types of racial discrimination. The message was now clear, and sometimes explicitly spelled out: 'they' must be treated decently once they were here, but every effort would be made to ensure that no more of them than could possibly be avoided would get here in future. They were, after all, a problem.

The coarsening of sensibilities, of politicians, of the press and of the public, created by the hysteria about 'immigration' is difficult to believe. I remember an incident just before one Christmas concerning a family of Indian children being looked after by their eldest sister, a teenage girl. Their parents had been removed from the country (or possibly not allowed to re-enter it, I forget now which); the children had been left stranded here. A Government Minister appeared on television to reassure an anxious public: 'I promise you I will get rid of them', he said. Not one newspaper made the obvious comment about room in the inn. In the minds of many people, the presence of a single non-white person whom it was possible to keep out or remove became a calamity greater than the death of thousands. The son of a Ghanaian government minister was studying at a college, supported by regular remittances from his father. One of the many coups occurred in Ghana, and the boy's father was imprisoned. The boy panicked: he stopped attending the college and took a job to support himself, although he was not legally entitled to do so. His absence was reported by the college, and he was arrested by the police. When his case came before a magistrate, the magistrate showed no understanding of the boy's plight or of his fear for his father and himself. Instead, he raged against the youth, telling him what a terrible thing he had done. The boy was sent to prison, with a recommendation for deportation when he had served his sentence. These are two of countless examples of behaviour of which you would think only a nation of sadists capable. It was not exactly sadistic behaviour: it was neurotic behaviour, induced by endless repetition, by press and politicians alike, of hysterical hate-propaganda.

Far worse was to come. In 1968 there arose a so-called crisis about Asians from East Africa. When the African territories had become independent countries, the British Government negotiated a deal whereby Asian residents had two years in which to decide whether to opt to become citizens of the new countries or to remain citizens of the UK and Colonies. Their decision would then be irrevocable. The deal was less favourable than that offered to white British expatriates; even if these chose to become citizens of the new states, their citizenship of the UK and Colonies would be restored to them if ever they came to regret their decision. The deal with the Asians was made in full awareness that, if they opted to remain citizens of the UK and Colonies, they would no longer be subject to control under the 1962 Commonwealth Immigrants Act, since their passports would not have been issued by colonial administrations, but by direct representatives of the British Government. A certain number chose to become citizens of the African countries, with the exception of Malawi, which did not allow them to do so, but had a nationality law based on African race. But a certain number elected to remain citizens of the UK and Colonies, fearful of discrimination under Africanisation policies by the governments of the countries in which they were living and confident that, in that case, they would be able to find a new home in the country which had offered them its citizenship. Those who had opted for British citizenship started to experience precisely such discrimination, especially in Kenya. They were dismissed from civil service posts; they were denied labour permits; they were not allowed to send their children to the state schools. They therefore began to exercise their right to come freely to Britain. The newspapers whipped up alarm. They were defined as 'immigrants', which, properly speaking, they were not: white people of British descent who exercised a similar right freely to enter a country whose citizens they were but which they had never seen were never described as 'immigrants'. What made our citizens from East Africa 'immigrants' was the colour of their skins. The Labour Government responded to the panic whipped up by the Press by manifesting equal panic; it committed the most shameful act of any British government since the War.

Unfortunately, Roy Jenkins, the only humane Home Secretary this century, had left the post for the Treasury, and had been succeeded by Jim Callaghan. A new Commonwealth Immigrants Bill was prepared, denying to British citizens from East Africa entry to the only country on the face of the globe in which they had had an unquestionable right to live. The Bill was rushed through both Houses of Parliament in a week flat. Numerous groups petitioned the Queen not to sign the Bill into law; it after all denied some of her subjects their rights. No use: she signed it without cavil. In introducing the Bill, Callaghan had spoken of 'solemn obligations' to those who were to be excluded. He did not mean that, because we had solemn obligations to them, we must not do to them what the Bill proposed to do. He meant that it was so important to keep them out that we must even flout solemn obligations. But he still refrained from specifying what made it important. Everyone was supposed to understand that without its being said. And they did. Indeed, in support of the Bill, Government Ministers could engage in the crudest racist propaganda. In the House of Lords, the Lord Chancellor, Lord Gardiner, gave the grossly exaggerated figure of two million citizens of the UK and Colonies in East Africa, saying of them:

> And all these people are entitled to arrive and go, I suppose, to Huddersfield or Bradford and say, 'You build the schools, and train, employ and pay the teachers to teach our children; you build the hospitals and find the doctors and nurses; we have a right to come here and you must find the houses'.[4]

A system of 'quota vouchers' was inaugurated. Asian citizens of the UK and Colonies living in the East African countries could apply for such vouchers – limited at first to 1,500 a year, increased in 1971 to 3,000 – and come to Britain if their applications succeeded. Those who came without a quota voucher were subjected to a cruel punishment: they were 'shuttle-cocked'. This meant that they were put back on to the planes on which they had arrived, which then made the return journey to where they had embarked. This was done in the full knowledge that they would be refused entry to the country from which they had fled. Very often they then had to stay on the plane for its further flight to Australia or other destination, and eventually all the way back to Britain. At that stage, they would then be again put back on the plane, to repeat the whole process: sometimes this happened three or more times. Finally, arrived yet once more in Britain, they would be placed in detention. Callaghan was an enthusiastic shuttlecocker, who did not hesitate to apply this punishment to women with children: women who held the British citizenship we had so generously offered to them when independence came. Naturally, the successor Conservative Government continued the same practice.

Despite the manifest racism that had motivated the rushing through Parliament of the 1968 Act, members of the Government that had done this terrible thing to some degree deceived themselves, and attempted to deceive others. David Ennals, Under-Secretary at the Home Office, expressed indignation at criticism from those opposed to racism: could they not understand that passing the Commonwealth Immigrants Act was the one essential step to ensure 'good race relations'? A Home Office official was sent to tour the race relations councils, who were aghast at what had happened, to explain to them what a great service the Government had done to race relations by bringing in the 1968 Act. They had stemmed racist feeling by appeasing it; no one now could doubt the Government's sincere intention to bring 'immigration' as nearly to an end as could be conceived; henceforward racist demands to stop 'immigration' would die away. The anger would cease, and, with it, the enmity. Of course, none of those to whom he talked heard him with anything but contempt. Even to those who believed in doing evil that good might come, the argument was so patently fallacious: it was the craven excuse of the evildoer anxious for absolution. It took very little time for events to expose the fallacy. The only consequence of surrender to malice is to inflame the malice, to whet the appetites of the malicious.

And yet the doctrine preached by apologists for the Act of 1968 has become a standard politicians' motto. It had been heard as early as 1966. At that time it was accompanied by the obviously false declaration that 'integration and immigration are two separate questions'. It was later to be encapsulated by the Conservatives in a jingle that linked immigration directly to race: 'Firm but fair immigration control is the key to good race relations'. The motto was taken over by the Labour party, whose last manifesto before the 1997 election announced its prospective immigration policy under the heading 'Firmer and Fairer', and whose White Paper announcing its coming Asylum and Immigration Bill was entitled 'Faster, Fairer and Firmer'. Only a fool could actually believe that the never-ending conduct of the immigration auction in such a manner would make for 'good race relations'. Quite the contrary. Every new political campaign for tighter immigration controls, every new set of allegedly scandalous revelations in the press about newly arrived immigrants, raised the racist temperature yet higher. The immigration auction kept racist feeling constantly on the boil.

In 1968 the politicians' silence about the motives for preventing 'coloured' people, whether genuinely immigrants or in fact our own citizens, from entering the country, supplied

Enoch Powell with his chance. If he were to spell out the reasons, left unspoken by the politicians but meant by them to be tacitly understood, he would become a hero to all the millions who were appalled by the presence of 'coloured' people in their midst; the political leaders could not say that what he said was untrue, or their political strategy would be wrecked, and their previous actions rendered absurd. The speech, larded with insulting terms such as 'piccaninnies' and with shameless and preposterous falsehoods, was flagrantly racist: Powell endorsed a constituent's prediction that 'in fifteen or twenty years the black man will have the whip hand over the white man'. Callaghan's reply could amount to no more than the plea that the Government *was* trying to keep Britain white; as Powell pointed out in his next speech on race, Heath's rebuke to him did not deny anything he had said, but merely reprimanded him for the language he used. Powell of course succeeded in arousing vehement public and private manifestations of racial hatred. But the principal culprits were the leaders of the Labour and Conservative parties, who had provided him with an opportunity to express the squalid emotions that so many nurtured, and had blocked themselves from being able to say that his statements were untrue.

With Powell's speech threatening that the Tiber would foam with blood, with the demonstration by dockers and a letter by forty immigration officers at Heathrow in support of it, with the subsequent speeches that Powell made on the same theme, and with the wholesale manifestations of racial hatred that they engendered, two things were now clear: the British public was desperately opposed to immigration; and by 'immigration' it understood only the entry of people with black or brown skins. Seven years of propaganda by politicians – not only rogue politicians such as Powell but the mainstream politicians of both major parties – and by the journalists and newspaper editors, too, had fixed those principles firmly in the minds, not indeed of all white members of the British public, but of a large majority.

It is just possible that some politicians believe the twaddle about firm and fair immigration controls as the key to good race relations, if indeed a politician can be said to believe anything but that such-and-such is the politically advantageous thing to say. What they really take harsh and unjust immigration rules to be the key to is electoral success. By 1968, the politicians of both major parties had convinced themselves that a lenient immigration policy would bring about a massive loss of votes; if you wanted to win elections, you must be tougher on immigration than the other lot. The two parties therefore began a protracted auction of immigration restrictions. Each party, when out of power, would accuse the other of admitting an excessive number of immigrants, and of publishing false statistics to disguise the fact. Each, arrived in power, would impose new and ever harsher restrictions. To be successful, this game with human lives demanded deception of the public. In 1971 a new Immigration Act was passed by the Heath government with the avowed purpose, to which Heath had personally pledged the Conservative Party in 1967, of bringing primary immigration to an end: there was some irony in the passage of such an Act at just the time when the same government was taking Britain into the European Community, thus allowing nationals of all member states free entry into Britain. 'Primary immigration' meant the arrival of heads of families who would be entitled to bring their wives and children; in fact, the restrictions on immigration from the Commonwealth imposed by the previous Labour administration were already so severe as to have reduced such primary immigration almost to nothing. The 1971 Act introduced into immigration law the blatantly racist concept of 'patriality', a status to be held by those born, registered or naturalised, or having a parent born, registered or naturalised in the UK.[5] After the Act came into force on New Year's Day, 1973, only those Commonwealth citizens who were patrial would have 'right of abode in the UK'. Non-patrials, like aliens, might still be able to become settled in the country, but would, like aliens, be granted citizenship only at discretion, and might be deported without the recommendation of a court. Essentially, then, non-patrial Commonwealth citizens were henceforward to be assimilated to (non-EC) aliens in our immigration law. Originally the Bill had granted patriality to those with one grandparent born or naturalised in the UK, but this provision was removed by Parliament; its effect was, however, restored by the immigration rules that came into force at the same time. These rules also imposed a means test on non-patrials wishing to send for dependants.

But the government's attempt, by means of the 1971 Immigration Act, to end once for all the racist clamour to 'stop immigration' was overtaken by a decision on the part of an African tyrant, Idi Amin of Uganda. On 4 August 1972 Amin announced that the Asians of Uganda had just three months to leave the country. Of these, many were citizens of the UK and Colonies, some citizens of Uganda and some stateless because they had applied for Uganda citizenship only after 25 January 1971. The immediate result in Britain was an outbreak of demands to refuse entry to the expelled Asians; Powell made speeches to propagate the lie that Britain had made no commitment to admit Asians with British citizenship. A large proportion of the British population supported the demand to 'Keep Them Out'. The question of what, even if Powell's mendacious claim had been sound, was to happen to these citizens of ours, expelled from the country where they had lived all their lives, in no way exercised the exclusionists; it seemed that, for all they cared, our Asian citizens could be dumped into the sea from the air, for certainly no other country had any duty to admit them. To its credit, the Heath government resisted the clamour and admitted expelled citizens of the UK and Colonies.

It was rightly done; but it was done with the least possible grace. The government pleaded with other countries to 'share the burden': India took 3,000 on a temporary basis, while Canada creamed off the most highly qualified. The weight of this burden can be judged from the fact that we eventually admitted 27,000 people: enough, as someone remarked, to fill a football stadium. Those wishing to come to Britain still had to obtain vouchers before they could board a plane: for fully half the three-month period during which they were required to leave, no vouchers were issued. When they were about to be, the British authorities issued leaflets to the Asians, telling them to avoid what they called 'red areas', meaning areas of Britain such as Leicester where there were already sizeable Asian communities which might provide support and would in some cases contain relatives of those expelled. When at last the vouchers were issued, they were restricted to those holding British passports: at first denied to women British citizens married to stateless men, they were later granted to them but not to their husbands; the Home Office callously remarked that it was usual for women to go wherever their husbands went.

Although by 1973, and effectively long before that, immigration from 'the new Commonwealth' had been reduced to the derisory trickle of those few wives and children who succeeded in convincing of their genuineness the entry certificate officers who routinely disbelieved anything said to them, the Ugandan crisis convinced the British public that floods were still pouring into the country: where people with brown or black skins were concerned, few members of that public could distinguish between British citizens and citizens of other Commonwealth countries, or between immigrants and refugees.

NOTES

1 Elspeth Guild, 'Immigration and Race – breaking the link', *Connections*, Summer 2000, CRE, p. 16.
2 Quoted from Ann Dummett and Andrew Nicol, *Subjects, Citizens, Aliens and Others*, Law in Context series, Weidenfeld and Nicholson, 1990, p. 180.
3 Quoted from Ann Dummett, *A Portrait of English Racism*, second edition, CARAF, 1984 (first edition 1973), pp. 235, 237.
4 *The Times*, 1 March 1968.
5 The full definition was slightly more complex, but the provision given here was the main one.

7

FROM IMMIGRANTS TO REFUGEES

In the summer of 1976, Britain experienced an outbreak of racial hysteria that seems scarcely believable now in 2000. It was ignited by the media, and industriously fanned by them throughout its whole appalling history. It began with the arrival of two hapless Goan families from Malawi. What had happened was that the Malawian radio was broadcasting one of the interminable speeches of the President, Dr Hastings Banda. In a Goan club, the radio was on, and a member said to one of the African club servants, 'Switch that damn thing off'. The servant happened to belong to Dr Banda's political party, and reported the incident. It came to the ears of the President, who was furious, and ordered that all those of Goan descent should be expelled from the country. The families that had arrived comprised the first victims of this expulsion. They were,

DOI: 10.4324/9781032641683-9

of course, citizens of the UK and Colonies, members of just that group which the 1968 Commonwealth Immigrants Act had barred from entry to the only country whose citizens they were. They had had no option of becoming citizens of Malawi, which reserved citizenship to those of sub-Saharan African race. Abruptly expelled from the country where they had been living all their lives, they had no choice but to come to Britain, even though the country of their citizenship denied them the right to do so.

They arrived on 29 March, with several small children, bereft of all their money and possessions: they had not been allowed to take anything out of the country with them. Hillingdon Council, which had the legal obligation to house them, since they had arrived at Heathrow, put them up, idiotically, or possibly with malice, in a four-star hotel, and gave them a quite inadequate amount of money to buy food and other necessary supplies. The *Daily Express* discovered this and on 4 May publicised it as a 'scandal': the destitute refugees from Dr Banda's Malawi became 'the Four-Star Immigrants'. Journalists descended on them to ask what they had come for: asked whether they appreciated British welfare services, they politely replied that they were excellent. This was translated into headlines as FOUR-STAR ASIANS JUST HERE FOR THE WELFARE. I remember watching BBC television with incredulity while it showed a BBC reporter browbeating the bewildered family with the question, 'Have you come for British welfare handouts?' Of course, they had come because there was nowhere else on God's earth where they could go. They had until then needed no welfare benefits: they had been reasonably prosperous people in Malawi, and they had had everything taken from them. Asked by one journalist whether they were being given enough money, they said that they did need rather more: in fact, the amount they were given came to minuscule sums for each person's meal. WE WANT MORE MONEY, SAY THE £600-A-WEEK ASIANS, blared the headline next day. After the campaign of indignation had been running for only a few days, they were removed from the hotel and transferred on 7 May to an old workhouse building. There they had to endure a contingent of the National Front marching round the former workhouse with banners, chanting 'Send Them Home'. If only they could have gone home, they must have thought.

That was our welcome to our own citizens, turned out of their home and the country where they had always lived: that was how Britain was determined to pay out 'immigrants' who committed the unspeakable crime of coming here, voluntarily or involuntarily. The furore whipped up by the media had an immediate effect in inflaming racist feeling. Asian women were spat at while they stood at bus stops; three Indian youths were murdered on the streets. Meanwhile other events took place to exacerbate the situation. In Leamington Spa a house was advertised for sale by a notice in front of it which said, 'No coloureds need apply'. This flagrant breach of the 1968 Race Relations Act was given massive publicity by the press, with tacit though not quite overt approval. The second Race Relations Act had been passed in the wake of the Commonwealth Immigration Act to appease anti-racist feeling, on the familiar principle, 'Keep them out, but treat them decently if they do get in'. It covered a wide range of types of racial discrimination, though with inadequate machinery for enforcement. Driven to rage at the rising tide of racism, and at the racist House for Sale advertisement, an Indian householder in Leamington Spa retaliated by putting up a sign advertising his own house for sale, with the qualification 'No whites need apply'. This, too, was given headline treatment; the reports of it were extremely hostile. Convinced that this act was only making a terrible situation worse, Dr Prem, one of the longest-settled of Indians in Britain, and a man deeply committed to combating racism, travelled to Leamington and prevailed upon the Indian householder to take down his sign. The news of this was given to the Associated Press and other agencies: not a single newspaper reported it. Meanwhile the original offender, Robert Relf, a member of the National Front, refused to take his notice down; he eventually went to prison for contempt of court, and the press made him a national martyr.

A few other Goan families were expelled from Malawi, making 109 people in all;[1] their arrival was duly reported on the front pages. A *Daily Express* headline said, 'Another 20,000 Asians on the Way'. The Joint Council for the Welfare of Immigrants sent one of its members to Malawi to investigate the matter. He reported that the only Asians under threat of expulsion were members of the small Goan community, and that the number of 40,000 Asians in Malawi given by the *Daily Mail*[2] ought to have been 5,000. The organisation accordingly wrote to the *Mail* asking for a correction. No correction was forthcoming. Instead, the editor, Mr (later Sir) David English, expressing a favourite right-wing myth, replied privately:

> Does it or does it not concern you that the ever-proliferating race relations industry, with its strident voice, aggressive attitudes and constantly increasing number of bureaucrats is resulting in the majority of the British people believing that there is a plot to enforce greater and greater immigration on this country?[3]

Meanwhile Enoch Powell had not been inactive. He started even before the first Goan family arrived in March, warning of the dangers of immigration in a speech in January. In April he told the Police Federation that mugging was a racial crime. In May he released a confidential report to the Foreign Office on the admission of dependants by a civil servant, one D. F. Hawley. The burden of this report was that there was not a finite pool of dependants of immigrants from the new Commonwealth waiting to be admitted: the pool was infinite, because dependants would in turn have dependants, who would have dependants of their own, who would have dependants . . . This argument, and indeed the whole report, displayed complete ignorance of the rules and of the facts: but it caused the greatest alarm, among the public and in Parliament. There an MP told the House that Powell had informed him that an immigration officer had told him, Powell, that the immigration service had received instructions from the Home Office to admit immigrants from the Indian subcontinent even if they had forged passports. It beggars belief that MPs can have listened with seriousness to such malicious nonsense; it testifies to Powell's dishonesty that he never repudiated it.

The National Front won a noteworthy number of seats in the local elections of May 1976. In response, the Anti-Nazi League was formed to oppose it; but, though it attracted support from a wedge of anti-racist groups and individuals, it was generally perceived as a movement of the far Left. The Labour Government responded in a different and by now traditional way: it tightened the immigration controls yet further. In 1977 the new immigration rules imposed new controls on the admission of husbands, and generally turned the screw still tighter on the admission of dependants; fees for overseas students were very sharply increased. The country generally lurched heavily towards the Right, and Control of Immigration figured prominently in the propaganda of the various think tanks that promoted the newly popular right-wing, free-market doctrines. Alfred Sherman, director of one of them, wrote in the *Daily Telegraph* for 9 September 1976 that 'the imposition of mass immigration from backward alien cultures' was part of an attack on 'all that is English and wholesome'.[4] No more concise illustration could be desired of the crassness, dishonesty and ignorance, real or feigned, of the pressure against 'immigration', or of its racist inspiration. It was standard among those demanding an end to 'immigration' to represent the arrival of British subjects from the Caribbean, the Indian sub-continent and East Africa, not merely as comprising enormous numbers, but as a policy deliberately 'imposed', for mysterious reasons, by successive British governments. The contrast between these new arrivals and the 'wholesome' English trades on the coarsest racial fantasies about purity and 'natives'. All who were part of the first wave of immigration from the West Indies testify that they were brought up to regard themselves as British, and taught at school that everyone in Britain would accept them as British: the shock of being taken as 'alien' and 'backward' ('Get back up the trees' was a common racist gibe) inflicted a deep psychological wound. As for the stupidity of describing Indian culture as 'backward', only in a country in which India first enters the history books as the subject of conquest by Britain could such nonsense fail to bring its perpetrator into derision.

We have seen that, by 1973, and in practice well before that, immigration from 'the new Commonwealth' had been reduced to the trickle of wives and children of those who were settled here, together with a few elderly parents and women coming to marry settled bridegrooms. Very far from all of those categories entitled to come succeeded: the infamous virginity tests no doubt kept out some prospective brides, as well as merely humiliating and shaming others; while careful impartial studies showed that a great proportion of wives and children who had been refused were perfectly genuine. But, for all that, the public still believed that 'immigrants' – meaning immigrants from the New Commonwealth, of course – were still flooding into the country. This illusion was advantageous for the two major parties. Each hoped to convince the public that the supposed floods were due to the carelessness and duplicity of the opposing party, and so to induce the electorate to vote for the party which promised even tighter restrictions than the other. Hence the true facts must be concealed from the public. Thus as late as the 1979 election campaign, two girls, interviewed in the street by a TV reporter, said that they could not understand why immigrants were still allowed to enter in their thousands: they plainly had no idea that primary immigration from the Commonwealth had been brought to an end many years before. How could they be expected to? The press carefully kept the fact from them, and the politicians were not anxious for it to be grasped by the general public; only those members of it who had followed the details of the immigration laws and regulations could have known better. Mrs Thatcher had famously warned that the immigrant floods would swamp our culture, and promised to avert the danger: surely she could not have been indulging in fantasy or a deliberate lie.

In early 1978 Mrs Thatcher, who had been elected leader of the Conservative Party in 1975, gave a celebrated interview on television in which she said that Britain was in danger of being 'really rather swamped' by people of a different culture. This was a bid, successful on the whole, as the general election in the following year showed, to cut the ground from under the National Front and attract the racist vote to the Conservatives. No threat to British culture from immigrants from the Caribbean or the Indian subcontinent existed: there was, and remains, a grave threat from the influence of the United States. Another purpose of the remark was to maintain the public's belief that 'immigration' was a menace to be warded off at all costs, and to encourage it to think that 'immigrants' continued to flood in, and that only the policies of the Conservative Party would put a stop to the flood. In fact, of course, all but the small number of wives and children who succeeded in persuading the entry certificate officers that they were 'related as claimed' had been blocked off for many years.

Mrs Thatcher said something else, too, in that interview. She said that, if immigration was not stopped, people would resent it and become rather angry. She thereby deliberately encouraged hostile feelings against Commonwealth immigrants already in the country, and flattered white people who nurtured such feelings that they were responding in a natural and patriotic way. This illustrated another constant feature of the political immigration game. All those who had from the start been hostile to the arrival of people of darker skins, or who had been induced by the unremitting pressure of propaganda from the politicians and the press to feel hostile to it, were flattered by being told that their feelings were proper and natural, that they had been betrayed and were quite right to be angry about the transformation of their environment by the presence of coloured people. This had been a constant feature of the pronouncements of politicians of the two major parties ever since the consensus on Commonwealth immigration had been formed in 1965. The public was never told that it should be ashamed of manifesting its racist feelings, or of harbouring them: it was told instead that resentment against the presence of coloured people was entirely understandable, that English people were entitled to have and express such feelings. Mrs Thatcher was only saying, in a characteristically more inflammatory manner, what all leading Conservative and Labour politicians had been saying for many years.

The aroused racism of the country was manifested during the general election of 1979 by a grave fracas at Southall on 23 April – St George's Day – of that year. Southall has of course a large Indian population; the local Indian Workers' Association owned the Dominion Cinema there. The National Front was putting up a candidate in the election, and Ealing Council had allowed it to hold a meeting in Southall Town Hall, obviously chosen, in place of anywhere else in the constituency, for its provocative effect. On the one day of the year when the St George's flag would have been more appropriate, the Union Jack, adopted by the National Front as its own symbol, flew over the Town Hall. Members of the local constituency were unable to get into the meeting: seats had been reserved for the Press and for numerous National Front supporters bussed in from outside. Ignoring previous discussions with community representatives, the police occupied in force all four streets leading from the central cross-roads: people arriving from work by bus or train found themselves unable to get home because their route was blocked by the police. Permission for a peaceful meeting of protest against the National Front had been promised, but it could not take place because the organisers could not contact one another across the police barricades.

Residents of Southall saw their town as subjected to the equivalent of a colonial occupation force; many viewed the massive police presence as a punitive expedition. The Anti-Nazi League had encouraged many of its supporters to come to Southall to protest against the National Front. Some violence against the police predictably ensued: many local residents, who had certainly neither planned nor engaged in any violence, or even intended to take part in any protest meeting, were caught up in the mêlée, trying to reach their homes. The violence offered to the police was well surpassed by the violence committed by the police themselves, who chased with their batons innocent people who had been committing no crime and made completely unnecessary charges with batons and riot shields. An officer of the TGWU said, 'I have never seen such unrestrained violence against demonstrators'. Newspaper reports relied principally on information given by the police, and claimed a far higher

number of policemen than of demonstrators among the injured: in fact, numbers were almost exactly equal.

The worst police violence occurred at a house which was
being used as a store for placards and a centre for medical treatment: the occupants, including the injured and those treating
them, were evicted from the house with great violence and
made to run the gauntlet of a line of police hitting and kicking
them; musical equipment in the house, belonging to a community group that normally used it, was smashed to pieces.
The police gave frequent vent to racist feelings, using terms like
'black bastard' and 'nigger bastard'; some in a bus wrote the NF
logo on the steamed-up window and held up an Ace of Spades.
Many people sustained head injuries: notoriously, one of them,
Blair Peach, died from a fractured skull. Though offering no
violence himself, he had been struck by one of a group of four
policemen. Which of them administered the fatal blow was
never established, but none was reprimanded or disciplined.

The principal action of the Conservative Government elected
in 1979 to appease demands for ever tighter immigration control was to pass a new Nationality Act, designed, as William
Whitelaw had explained in 1978, 'to reduce future sources of
primary immigration'.[5] The Act, introduced in 1981 and coming into effect on 1 January 1983, abolished the old status of
Citizen of the UK and Colonies, replacing it with three new
types of citizenship. Only one of these, that of British Citizen,
conferred the right of abode in Britain. The other two were Citizenship of the British Dependent Territories, for those living in
the few remaining colonies, and British Overseas Citizenship.
It was into this last category that the remaining British citizens
in East Africa were now bundled; promised British citizenship
with the right of entry to Britain when the countries where
they were living became independent, but denied the right of
abode in Britain by the 1968 Commonwealth Immigrants Act,

their hope of eventually obtaining the 'quota vouchers' that had been being slowly doled out to them was finally extinguished. Neither of these two classes of citizenship gave to their holders the right of abode anywhere on the planet: not in the colonies or countries where they were living, their right to live in which would depend on the laws of those colonies or countries. As was widely observed, the Act translated immigration categories into categories of citizenship. In the same Act, the immemorial principle of *ius soli* – the right to British citizenship of anyone born on the territory – was abolished: henceforth this would apply only to those one of whose parents was either a British citizen or permanently settled.

For purposes of the European Union, a British national was subsequently defined to be either a British citizen or a British Dependent Territories' citizen through connection with Gibraltar. The latter soon effectively obtained all the rights of British citizens; of course the Moroccan workers who had done so much to build up the colony obtained no such rights. In April 1983 full British citizenship was conferred upon the inhabitants of the Falkland Islands. Gibraltar and the Falkland Islands were the only dependencies with white populations: the racial line between those holding full British citizenship and those holding the inferior varieties was thus yet more clearly drawn. Although the term 'British subject', in its old connotation, was abolished, civic rights for those living in Britain were not attached to the new British citizenship, but continued to depend on citizenship of some Commonwealth country or dependency: hints were dropped that this might be rescinded, but, happily, it has not been.

It is highly inappropriate that a country that now routinely acknowledges that it will in perpetuity have a multi-racial population should have been saddled with a nationality law of great complexity, recognising five categories of Britishness (including British Protected Persons and a very small category to which the old name of 'British Subject' was transferred). Only one of these categories carries any rights. The new nationality law was based upon the desire to exclude all possible immigrants from outside the European Union and discriminated upon racial lines; yet, with all the talk of constitutional reform, there has been little hint of amending it. While Hong Kong remained a colony, politicians fantasised that, if given the right to do so, all the two and a half million inhabitants who were BDTCs (British Dependent Territories Citizens) might come to Britain before it was handed back to China; now that it has been handed back, even the most paranoid can give no serious reason why all the categories of British citizenship should not be amalgamated into one and awarded equal rights. (Full British citizenship was awarded in 1998 to the small number of British Dependent Territories Citizens who had no other nationality, thus excluding all from Hong Kong; the unfortunate British Overseas Citizens remain as before.) Of course, for all the racial motivation underlying the Nationality Act, there could be no question of depriving of full citizenship British citizens of Asian or Afro-Caribbean descent if they were resident in the country; but Britain has still been lumbered with a nationality law inspired by the sentiment 'We must keep Them out'.

Since 1983, however, the surge in racist feeling which began in 1976 has markedly subsided. It has subsided much as the tide does when it retreats from the rocks. Some of the rocks quickly dry in the sun: a fair section of the white British public, perhaps a quarter, possibly even more, has altogether lost its feelings of racial superiority, of contempt or hatred for people of other races; the proportion is higher among young adults than among the middle-aged and elderly. In clefts of the rock, deep rock pools remain: there are still within the white population pockets of rabid racists, suffused with feelings of hatred for those of a different colour and eager to do them all the harm they can. These are responsible for racist attacks and racist murders, of which the most celebrated is that of Stephen Lawrence, for windows smashed and burning rags stuffed through letter boxes, for children taunted and ridiculed on their way to school, for beatings up in police vans or police stations: for insensate hatred that causes unending misery for some, in other words. And there are patches of rock still covered with soaking, slimy seaweed. A large section of the white British public is still imbued with racist prejudices. Its members would not descend to violence, but would make hurtful jokes to or about people from the racial minorities, would deny them jobs or promotion whenever they thought they could do so without being detected as practising racial discrimination, would arrest them for no good reason or sentence them more harshly than white offenders, or would treat them with hostility or contempt when in some position of authority. Such people are responsible for the continuing high level of discrimination in employment and the high proportion of black people in the prisons; in everyday life, they can make their victims' lives unbearable or wretched. Unhappily, but unmysteriously, they are attracted to occupations which heavily impinge upon the lives of members of the ethnic minorities: immigration officers and the police (an effect the police are now, at very long last, counteracting).

It is difficult to estimate what proportions of the white British population make up these three categories. One can make only impressionistic assessments. An optimistic guess might place the category corresponding to the sun-dried rock, now quite weaned from racial prejudice (and unconscious of ever having felt it), as high as 25 per cent. The denizens of the rock pools – the still virulent racists – probably make up about 15 per cent. Those comparable to the wet seaweed – strongly racist but not taking part in physical persecution – will then form about 60 per cent of the total white population – far too many for a healthy multi-racial society, but an improvement on the state of affairs in 1976. They must have made up the majority which voted to exonerate Enoch Powell in the television debate referred to in Chapter 6. And yet, despite these depressing estimates, Britain has succeeded in making itself genuinely into what it had long been being told that it was – a multi-racial society. That cannot yet be said of many other European countries.

This gradually altering atmosphere did not curtail the Conservative Government's efforts to block immigration from outside the European Union. By changes in the administrative rules, it limited the access of immigrants to health care, education, council housing and welfare benefits. The Immigration Act of 1988 removed the statutory right of Commonwealth citizens, including British citizens, to be joined by a husband or wife; it also withdrew from most of those threatened with deportation the right to challenge the order before an independent court or tribunal. In August 1988 the automatic right of MPs to make representations on behalf of people refused entry was withdrawn. Every new restriction was justified by the wearyingly repeated slogan 'Fair but firm immigration control is the key to good race relations', encapsulating the political policy that had provoked the continual worsening of race relations for two decades from 1961 onwards. But there was also a change of direction. Government policy came to be directed as much against refugees as against immigrants, two completely different categories of people. The Conservative Government, followed in this by its Labour successor, did its utmost to blur the distinction, not only referring constantly to 'bogus asylum-seekers' but frequently describing them as 'economic migrants', as 'illegal immigrants' or as 'abusing the system'.

Why this partial switch of attention from immigrants to refugees? For many years, the two major parties had been playing a game with the voting public, colluding with each other to give the impression that a flood of coloured immigrants was still pouring into the country, and each assuring voters when it came to power that its new restrictive measures would at last stem the flood that the opposing party had failed to withstand. This game was being played long after all primary immigration had been brought to a halt. But doubtless the idea filtered into the politicians' minds that the game could not continue to be played indefinitely; perhaps the voters might begin to suspect that a game was being played with them, and that there was no flood to be stemmed. It would be disastrous for the politicians to be caught out in deceiving the public. But Conservative and Labour politicians were both convinced of two things. First, that the propaganda of the past three decades had ensured that there were votes to be gained by being tough on immigration, and votes to be lost by being soft on it. And, secondly, that the public mind had been thoroughly imbued with the belief that the admission of a single person whom there was any means of keeping out was an unparalleled disaster. For these reasons, it would not pay the politicians to declare that there was no longer any danger of unwanted arrivals to be averted. Refugees made an apposite substitute for immigrants. For one thing, unlike immigrants, they palpably existed; indeed, with persecution and inner conflicts increasing throughout the world, their numbers were increasing. The hostility to people entering the country from other lands engendered by the decades-long propaganda by politicians and media was no longer, as it had been in the first instance, a pure expression of racial prejudice: it now stood on its own, and, as a separable prejudice, had been detached from the racial prejudice from which it had sprung. It could therefore be directed against any group which politicians and media combined to depict as a threat; and of course most of the media are only too ready to stir up hostility towards any group of people the politicians wish the public to be hostile to.

That there is much truth in these assumptions was shown by the arrival at Dover of a group of Gypsies from the Czech Republic claiming asylum. This occurred shortly after the great manifestation of national grief at the death of Princess Diana. The outpouring of grief was diagnosed by many commentators as the birth of a gentler, more compassionate attitude; the reaction to the arrival of the Gypsies gave the lie to this interpretation. There is good evidence that Gypsies are indeed persecuted in the Czech Republic: they are treated with hostility by the general population and harshly by officialdom, and many have been stripped of their citizenship. No compassion was shown them by the people of Dover, who displayed undisguised hostility; a National Front march demanding their expulsion was welcomed by many. The Home Office quickly returned them to the Czech Republic without making any serious effort to consider their claims to asylum.

The first move in the Government's campaign to clamp down on refugees was to impose visa requirements on people coming from countries from which many were likely to flee, seeking asylum elsewhere. Thus visas were demanded of Iranians in 1980, and in 1985 a visa requirement was imposed virtually overnight on people coming from Sri Lanka, from which many Tamils had been escaping to claim asylum in other countries, and particularly in Britain. Intending asylum-seekers who had booked their passages for the next day found themselves suddenly prohibited from boarding their flights. How far Britain had now moved from the principle of free entry of British subjects that held good up to 1962! Since then, visas have been demanded of travellers from several other Commonwealth countries, including Uganda, Sierra Leone, Tanzania and Kenya; they are required also of those coming from Turkey and most of former Yugoslavia.

It is obvious that people fleeing persecution are very badly placed to obtain visas; they are lucky if they are already in

possession of passports. The British Government is uncon-
cerned to offer refuge to the persecuted: its operations are carried out with the purely cynical purpose of seeing that as few
of the persecuted as possible can contrive to reach Britain to ask
for refuge. That is manifest from the second move, the Carriers'
Liability Act of 1987, which imposed a fine of £1,000 per head
on air or shipping lines for each passenger arriving without
papers fully in order: airline staff members were thereby converted into surrogate immigration officers. In 1991 the fine
was doubled to £2,000 per head. It may be imposed even if the
individual concerned is granted asylum: the principle is clearly
to prevent from reaching Britain even those with a claim which
the system would recognise as valid. Almost all European countries have now adopted similar measures: Britain led the way.
Under the Asylum and Immigration Act 1999, the penalty may
be imposed, not just on airlines, but on operators of any means
of transport, such as lorry drivers, whether they are aware of
carrying passengers or not.

The third device British governments have adopted for dis-
couraging asylum-seekers has been to lock them up. A large
number are detained, either in detention centres like Campsfield House near Oxford, especially designed for the purpose,
or in actual prison, the detention centres being unable to accommodate all who are subjected to detention. The official excuse for doing this is that those locked up might otherwise
abscond, going to ground so that the authorities cannot remove them when their applications for asylum are denied.
Since a large number are detained immediately after they make
their original applications for asylum, it seems extremely unlikely that this is the real reason in most cases: as is very generally supposed, detention is intended as a deterrent to dissuade
potential future asylum-seekers. Those detained are given no
reason for being shut up in detention centre or prison, and

have no legal means of challenging the detention order against them. They do not know why they have been shut up, and, although they are allowed to contact lawyers, they have no information about how their applications are doing. These unfortunates languish in their prisons or detention centres, not knowing why they are there, how long they will be there or what their eventual fate will be; at Campsfield, they are not in the charge of Government servants, but of the employees of a private security firm, Group 4, to which custody of them has been allotted. The number of those detained has been rising steadily year by year; at the time of writing there are about 1,000 in detention.

Under the Asylum and Immigration Act 1999 introduced by the Labour Government, the deterrent measures were made harsher yet. Asylum-seekers are to be dispersed around the country, regardless of whether there is anyone of their language or nationality in the place to which they were sent; they could refuse to go, but on pain of losing all support in money, kind or accommodation. They will no longer be eligible for social security benefits. They are to be supported, at 70 per cent of the income support benefit allotted to citizens, a level well below the minimum considered necessary for subsistence; and the support will be distributed, not in money, but in the form of vouchers, which they will be able to spend only at designated stores, and which will make them instantly identifiable as asylum-seekers. In a final twist whose meanness defies belief, if they offer vouchers higher in value than the goods they are buying, the store will be required by the Government to keep the change. The number of those put into detention is to be greatly increased. Despite these measures, the Conservative opposition attacks the Government for making Britain a 'soft touch' for refugees, and puts out its own propaganda about 'floods' of bogus asylum-seekers.

At the same time, the Government, with its Home Secretary Jack Straw in the lead, keeps a constant stream of propaganda flowing against bogus asylum-seekers and the need to keep them out of the country and deter the evil traffickers in human misery who bring them here. From what misery can these 'traffickers' be being paid to rescue people? The question is never asked. It is hard to answer while maintaining that those who pay them are all – or even almost all – fraudulent. Presumably the answer would have to be that they are mere economic migrants, the misery that they are seeking to escape therefore being unbearable poverty, inability to feed their children and the like, with which we need have no concern. Rhetorical clichés are all; reason and compassion are discarded.

The effect of all this could have been predicted by the merest ninny; yet when Bill Morris, General Secretary of the Transport and General Workers' Union, points it out, Jack Straw professes to be mystified by his remarks. The effect, mounting to a crescendo as I write, has been both to stimulate and to expand the racism which still festers amongst the white British public. It has expanded it from a loathing of and contempt for 'coloured people' to a loathing of and contempt for foreigners in general, including white foreigners – more exactly, poor white foreigners; it has expanded racism proper into xenophobia, in other words. The popular press, national and local, has incited its readers to violent hatred of supposedly 'bogus' refugees, the local paper in Dover calling them 'the scum of the earth'; a large percentage of the white population, incited by the newspapers and encouraged by the evident sympathy of the Government and the opposition for their views, has now absorbed this new poison. Those who find it natural to express their opinions by violence no longer restrict their violent attacks to black people; unsurprisingly, Dover has experienced many such attacks upon asylum-seekers, and the Government has responded, not by rebuking the offenders, but only by promising to disperse asylum-seekers from Kent to other parts of Britain. With this, the tide of racist feeling of the familiar sort is mounting, despite the check it received from the Stephen Lawrence enquiry. Yet there is a difference from the earlier period: opposition to racism and xenophobia, and to the political policies that inflame them, dares now to make itself heard, where before it was voiced only by small dedicated anti-racist groups. A powerful and respected Trade Unionist has spoken out; and along with the faithful but woefully uninfluential Liberal Democrat Party, two national newspapers, the *Independent* and the *Guardian*, have consistently opposed the Government's asylum policy.

The processing of applications for asylum is extremely slow, although appeals against refusal are allowed; the narrowest of criteria for granting asylum are applied. It has happened several times that a refugee whose application has been refused and who has not even been granted Exceptional Leave to Remain has been sent back to his own country and there arrested, tortured or killed. Policies intended to prevent refugees even arriving to apply for asylum and to grant it to those who succeed in doing so as sparingly as possible are now common to almost all countries of the European Union: there is a consensus among most of the governments that refugees constitute a menace and must be kept out as resolutely as possible. The future in this respect is very difficult to predict. If there does come to be an immigration and asylum policy common to the whole European Union, it may well be more liberal than the policies of most of the member states; but that, too, is uncertain. European attitudes generally to immigration, race and refugees, and British attitudes to them in particular, are now in an unstable condition. The bulk of the populations of countries of the Union, supported in effect by their governments, is, though to some degree shamefacedly, hostile to foreigners, especially those from outside the Union, and to admitting them within the borders; but in all those countries there is a resolute minority determined to resist racism and xenophobia and to oppose the exclusionist policies that underpin them. It is difficult to say whether these minorities will be able to overcome the great force of prejudice and overturn the hostility to incomers that now informs most European countries' immigration and asylum policies, at the same time establishing genuinely multicultural societies. They may possibly do so, as demographic factors make immigration an ever greater necessity.

Meanwhile, the existing state of affairs is calamitous. It very clearly illustrates the inappropriateness to the present highly internationalised political and economic systems prevailing on the planet of sovereign nation-states concerned only with the interests of their own nationals. Governments and peoples of the existing nation-states – none more than those of Britain – clamour that their sovereignty must be retained and respected, and that they must be able to control their own frontiers; regional associations like the EU apply the same principle to themselves, concerning themselves only with their own. The plainly correct principle of subsidiarity, misinterpreted by British governments as laying down that centralised national governments should have total control, rules that problems should be dealt with at the lowest appropriate level. Yet, in to-day's world, there are many problems which can be handled effectively only by an international authority, to which all states ought to surrender authority in the matter concerned. An obvious example is the relief of parts of the world struck by one of the many natural disasters which now afflict us: earthquakes, tidal waves, volcanic eruptions and famine, even when the last is due to human actions more than to natural forces.

A far more controversial example is provided by claims on the part of some region of a country to independence from that country, for example of Biafra and of Bangladesh, of Tibet and of the Tamil region of Sri Lanka. The pressing of such claims and the determination of national governments to resist them has been the cause of many vicious civil wars; only Czechoslovakia and the Soviet Union avoided this outcome, the one by allowing the Slovak Republic to secede peacefully from its Czech partner, the other by acquiescing in the break-up of the Union into its component republics – a prudence since negated by the brutal attack upon the Chechens. Most recently, and most horribly, the disintegration of Yugoslavia was accompanied by horrifying war, massacres, rape and cruelty. By what criteria should it be decided whether some region within a country deserves to become independent? In the absence of any higher authority to judge between the parties, it is not generally decided by any criteria at all, only by the force that the central government can muster against the region and any external powers that choose to come to its assistance. Such conflicts are exacerbated by the doctrine of the sovereignty of the nation-state: the country faced with a demand for secession is not moved solely by economic factors, but often nurtures an almost religious devotion to its own integrity. If the country were part of some larger unit such as the European Union, and if the principle of subsidiarity already allowed a large measure of autonomy to the region claiming the right to secede, both the desire for secession and the resistance to it would be greatly weakened. But such circumstances would not silence all demands for independence: feelings of not being accepted or treated as full citizens or of being exploited for the benefit of the dominant group would still prompt such demands. The resolution of such disputes would be far better achieved by the judgements of an international body than by force, with its inevitable death and destruction even when not accompanied by atrocities. It should be evidently to the advantage of all that a body to adjudicate these quarrels should be set up, and that all nations should agree to abide by its decisions, rather than their being resolved by bloodshed which takes no account of the justice of the claim to secede. Such an international tribunal could decide on relevant rational grounds: how distinct from the majority in culture, language, religion and race the would-be seceders were; to what extent, if any, they were currently denied a full sense of sharing in the national identity; whether the region, if independent, would be economically viable; and so forth. Every decision the tribunal made would leave one party or the other aggrieved; some decisions would be mistaken. Yet the creation of such an international adjudicating body, by whose decisions all agreed in advance to abide, would obviously be so preferable to the present invitation to armed conflict that only obstinate adherence to the malign principle of national sovereignty can explain why no effort is initiated to adopt it.

Among problems that can be dealt with justly and effectively only on the international level is that of refugees. It will not subside: it can only swell. In the condition into which we have caused the world to sink, there is gross inequity in the wealth of countries, and many countries suffer from harshly repressive regimes, some tolerated by the West, some supplied by it with arms, some that have been actively encouraged by it. A great many such regimes routinely practise torture. The world free-market economy is teetering on the edge of collapse; suddenly impoverished residents of countries whose economy has broken down launch physical attacks upon hapless ethnic minorities which they blame for their plight. As long as these conditions persist, huge waves of refugees will stream from this country and from that, and, since the air transport system makes it possible and Western economies still flourish, most will head for the West. That will not make them 'economic migrants only wanting to better themselves': most will still be escaping intolerable conditions or genuine persecution, and will naturally make for countries in which they believe they will have a chance of supporting themselves. Until these world conditions are remedied, of which there is little sign, the phenomenon of the mass exodus of refugees is likely to intensify.

So far, it has been only poor countries – Ethiopia, Sudan, Pakistan – that have during crises in neighbouring countries accommodated vast influxes of a million or more refugees: European countries seize and remove tiny numbers when they present themselves. Can we watch the refugee totals swell, while Britain and other European countries turn their backs? Not only European countries indeed: it is not long since Malaysia bundled its Indonesian immigrants back to their country, reportedly subjecting them to some ill treatment as a prelude to expulsion. If the countries of the European Union succeed in erecting a fortress which no one fleeing from persecution can breach, will we complacently watch from our safe vantage-point great tides of would-be refugees wash about the world, turned away from one country and then another, drowning as ramshackle boats go down, or incarcerated for years as were the wretched boat people in Hong Kong before being packed off by force to the land from which they fled? Has that antipathy to people wanting to enter which we have been imbibing from politicians eager to secure cheap votes and journalists who find it easier to arouse hatred than pity turned our hearts as stony as this? Surely not. But, if not, we must seek some means of dealing with the problem realistically and equitably, instead of thoughtlessly supporting the politicians in their strategies of exclusion.

Signatories, such as Britain, to the Geneva Convention on Refugees, are already bound to consider the claims of genuine seekers after asylum; they are also bound not to punish them for having inadequate documentation, though, contrary to international law, British courts have sentenced refugees for presenting invalid passports. Britain aims to comply with the provisions of the Convention, but interprets them in as minimalist a fashion as possible, and uses every device to prevent refugees from getting here to ask for asylum. No solution to the refugee problem can be expected from individual governments or their representatives acting in concert. National governments can be expected to act only in their national interests, or in a manner to please national voters; they will consult the interests of other countries only in so far as they coincide with their own. The problem of refugees can be solved only by the agreement of all countries to abide by the decisions of an international authority, which might be the existing UN High Commission for Refugees or some newly created body. Each country acceding to the agreement would rescind all measures intended to prevent applicants for asylum from arriving at its shores or frontiers. It would also consent to allow them to be interviewed by agents of the international authority, who would decide, on grounds independent of the policies of the country concerned, whether they had a genuine claim for asylum or not. The asylum-seekers, in turn, would agree in advance, if their claims were admitted, either to go to whatever country the international authority assigned them to or to return to their own country. This would of course require some amendment of the Geneva Convention, which implicitly requires that a genuine refugee must be admitted to the country where he first applies for asylum unless he can find some other country willing to accept him. The international authority would assign accepted refugees to countries party to the agreement under which it was operating in accordance with the resources of those countries, the wishes of the applicant and the suitability of the applicant, by reason of language, occupation, the whereabouts of relatives and so forth. Very likely this would result both in the acceptance of more claimants to asylum than are now accepted by Western countries and the allocation of more of them to those countries than they now admit. It would therefore require a degree of altruism, or a strong sense of justice, on their part to sign any such agreement. The alternative is, however, horrifying to contemplate. Indeed, the present situation is already horrifying.

Meanwhile, a ray of hope has pierced the gloom. It was announced on 21 July 2000 that Barbara Roche, Minister for Immigration, is to declare a volte-face on immigration by the British Government, which has plans to admit primary immigrants with specialist skills in health and information technology.[6] If these plans are realised, the dogma to which most British politicians have subscribed for three decades, that immigration is a threat which must be resisted by every means, will have been jettisoned: a quite new rhetoric, depicting immigrants as a benefit to the receiving country instead of a threat to it, has already started to be used. The move shows that the Labour Government has begun to wake up to the real demographic needs of the country. No doubt the traducing of asylum-seekers, the measures to prevent them from arriving and their harsh treatment when they do, will continue; a clear distinction between immigrants and refugees will again be recognised, to the detriment of the latter. An initial easing of the barriers against immigration, perhaps leading to a further easing yet, will reduce the pressure to apply for asylum as the only way of getting into the country, and may by this means lessen both official and unofficial clamour to stem the flow of aspirants to refuge.

NOTES

1 Peter Evans, *Publish and be Damned?*, Runnymede Trust, 1976, p. 18n.
2 *Daily Mail*, 10 May 1976, p. 11. The *Mail* had added that 'an exodus of Asians from Malawi is gathering force'.

3 JCWI Annual Report 1975–6, p. 2.
4 Ann Dummett and Andrew Nicol, *Subjects, Citizens, Aliens and Others*, Weidenfeld & Nicolson, London, 1990, p. 238.
5 Ann Dummett and Andrew Nicol, *Subjects, Citizens, Aliens and Others*, London, 1990, p. 241.
6 The *Independent*, 21 July 2000, p. 1.

8

RACISM IN OTHER EUROPEAN COUNTRIES AND IMMIGRATION INTO THEM

Britain has not been the only European country in which racism has infected sections of the public and put pressure upon politicians; nor has it been the only European country in which politicians, journalists, and members of the public have manifested hostility towards immigrants and asylum-seekers and accepted hysterical estimates of their numbers. Naturally, these phenomena have differed in character and intensity in accordance with the differing histories and circumstances of the various countries. But the last decade of the twentieth century has been generally marked in continental Europe by the tightening of immigration laws, under pressure from popular clamour

DOI: 10.4324/9781032641683-10

and from political parties of the extreme Right, and by a rapid acceleration of violent crimes against racial minorities.

Heavy immigration to France, mainly from other parts of Europe such as Poland, Czechoslovakia and Italy, took place between the two World Wars: about a quarter of the French population has some foreign ancestry. After 1945 the process of immigration into France became highly bureaucratised. France made bilateral agreements with Spain, Portugal and the North African countries to admit temporary workers in set numbers. These did not work well, and the French demand for labour outstripped the agreements: the result was massive illegal immigration to which French governments turned a blind eye. Thus twenty years ago migrant labour formed 80 per cent of the workforce in the Renault car works just outside Paris. Workers were admitted only for a temporary stay under the bilateral agreements, but were allowed to apply for a renewal of their permits, although the process of obtaining them was very bureaucratic.

From 1972 onwards French immigration policy has become much more restrictive, in large part in response to political pressure from the far Right; the economic crisis provoked by the rise in the price of oil had the same effect at this time in other European countries, where the far Right emerged as a menace somewhat later. French attitudes to racism differ greatly from British ones. The traditional assumption is that French culture coincides with civilisation: this was borne out in the French colonies, when they existed; the policy was to educate the inhabitants to become as like the French as possible. Race and colour were, at least in principle, irrelevant: what mattered was how deeply you had imbibed French culture. For this reason, French people are convinced that they are not racist (a conviction that sits uneasily with the sad history of French anti-Semitism). French anti-racism is to a large extent theoretical:

it concentrates on verbal expressions of racial prejudice. Thus, although an anti-racist law has been in force since 1972, only feeble attempts have been made in most places to enforce its provisions against racial discrimination in housing and employment. Combating such discrimination is made harder by the prevalent conviction that keeping records of people's race, as demanded by opponents of racism in Britain and the United States, is itself racist; it is against the law to categorise people by race for any official purpose. Moreover, cultural and religious triumphalism is regarded as quite compatible with racial justice. Prejudice against Islam, much inflamed in Britain by the Rushdie affair, is probably the most virulent and dangerous form of group hostility throughout Europe today; but in France it is widely shared by Right and Left. The Right hate Islam as an enemy of Christianity; the Left, including many committed anti-racists, hate it for the same reason as that for which they hate Christianity, because it is a religion. A manifestation of this is the refusal to allow Muslim girls to wear headscarves to school: the utterances of French headmasters on this subject are often bigoted, ignorant and cruel. Of course a great many immigrants to France, above all from Algeria, are Muslim, and see the hostility to their religion as of a piece with the strictly racial prejudice which they encounter: contempt for one's religion and actions that prevent one from practising it are actually more hurtful than prejudice against one's race or descent. But to most left-wing French people alert to the need to oppose racism, this would be a perplexing thought.

Algerians, to whom the police are particularly hostile, form the most visible racial minority in France, or at least that towards which there is the greatest hostility; there have been many instances of racial violence against them. North African immigrants are particularly concerned with the poor housing in which they have to live; they and other immigrants live in terror of being sent back to their countries of 'origin', which some of them have never seen, and are very reluctant to approach the police, even to report crimes committed against them, for fear this may happen to them. Meanwhile, the immigration laws have become progressively more severe. In 1972 the extreme right-wing group, Ordre Nouveau, set up the Front National as its parliamentary wing, and launched its campaign against immigrants; and in that year new harsher immigration controls were duly introduced. The Bonnet law of 1980 made it easier to deport illegal immigrants; and in September 1986 the first of the Pasqua laws was passed. This gave Prefects the power to order anyone deemed an illegal immigrant, without the right of any judicial defence or appeal, to be escorted to the frontier and expelled, reduced the categories of foreigners protected against removal and increased the documentation needed for entry into France. In 1993 new Pasqua laws withdrew the right to work from asylum-seekers and imposed sanctions on carrying companies; they deprived of the right to benefit anyone whose status was in any way irregular, for instance by a failure to file documents at the right time, even if he had been contributing to national insurance for years; they rescinded the right of those who had come to France as children to remain in France upon reaching majority. The rules about acquiring French citizenship were altered with retrospective effect, leaving people who had believed themselves French citizens and had been treated as such uncertain whether they still were or not, and scared to enquire for fear of being removed. The French state had declared war on immigrants.

A telling example of this war has been quoted by Colette Smith.[1] Unsurprisingly, it concerns Gypsies, who are always treated worse than anybody else. In 1995 thirteen families of Romanian Gypsies arrived in Lyons and were rounded up by the police without being given the chance to apply for asylum;

the men were sent to a detention centre, the women to a Salvation Army hostel and some of the children separated from their parents. The police interviewed them all, at a time when all the offices from which they could have obtained forms to apply for asylum were closed, and told them they would be taken back to the frontier. Lawyers acting for a voluntary organisation contested the decision, as contrary to the Geneva Convention. The men were brought to court handcuffed behind their backs, with chains held by police officers; in this condition, and with all in tears and, unable to understand French, perplexed about what was happening, they were reunited with their wives just before the court hearing, when the handcuffs were removed. The next day the judge ruled in favour of the Prefect's decision to refuse entry and return them to the frontier; while the lawyers were considering a further appeal, a plane carrying asylum-seekers arrived from Paris, picked up the Gypsies and flew them back to Romania. It has become a regular practice in EU countries, Britain included, to return Gypsy asylum-seekers to Eastern Europe without considering their cases. It is unsurprising that on 26 February 2000 leaders of the Roma community in the Czech Republic demanded compensation from the state because continual violation of their human rights had forced Roma to leave the country to seek refuge elsewhere.[2]

Germany does not regard itself as a country of immigration. Yet, immediately after the Second World War, West Germany received a massive number of immigrants, who contributed to a large degree to the celebrated 'economic miracle': some nine million people from East Germany moved into the western half of the divided country before the Berlin Wall went up. When it did, a large demand for labour continued. It was met by the importation of a great many people from other parts of Europe and from Asia Minor, intended to be merely temporary immigrants: the so-called guest workers – Yugoslavs, Greeks,

Portuguese, Italians and above all Turks (including Kurds from Turkey). This was good financially for the guest workers, but not in any other way: they had no rights. Since Germany does not allow dual nationality, they could not acquire German citizenship however long they stayed, save at the cost of forfeiting the citizenship of their homelands, which they have been deeply reluctant to do. They have been able to join trade unions, and IG Metall, in particular, has been very active on their behalf. But the general public has largely been unfriendly. There has been especial hostility to Turks, sometimes openly justified by their being of a different religion; as if, despite the national guilt for the Holocaust, no lesson had been drawn from the blossoming under Hitler of anti-Semitism into systematic massacre. It is not only Turks and Kurds who have suffered from German xenophobia, however: Italians and all other foreigners have experienced hostility from native Germans.

The rise in racial violence in Germany from 1991 onwards is notorious. It was inaugurated in that year – one in which there had been an emotional public discussion of refugees coming into Germany and of the law on asylum – by the horrible attack in the east German town of Hoyerswerda by neighbours and youths on a hostel for refugees; the refugees were then removed from the hostel, a result which caused those who had taken part in the attack or approved of it to count it as a success. This 'success' prompted further such attacks elsewhere: thus in August 1992 arson was committed against a reception centre for asylum-seekers in Rostock, and on 29 May 1993 another arson attack took place in Solingen on a house inhabited by Turks, five of whom were burned to death.[3] Among the German population are many resolute opponents of racism and xenophobia; but they do not determine the prevailing atmosphere. A report by Amnesty International in 1995 implicated the police, saying that 'a clear pattern of maltreatment of foreigners and ethnic minorities by the police is visible'; hardly any cases brought against the police for such offences succeed.

The Basic Law of the German Federal Republic (West Germany) enshrined a principle going back to the time of Bismarck: anyone of German descent, wherever living and however remote in time his or her German ancestry, was already a citizen of the Republic, on condition of acknowledging membership of the German people and possessing a basic knowledge of German language and culture. Under the treaty of reunification, all citizens of the German Democratic Republic (East Germany) automatically acquired citizenship of the newly reunified country. But the Basic Law provided for the citizenship of many more who were living outside any German territory: descendants of Germans who had emigrated to Romania in the thirteenth century, and of those who had gone to Russia under Catherine the Great, and enclaves exiled by Stalin to Central Asia. Many of these elected to transfer themselves to reunified Germany, and had no process of naturalisation to undergo: as soon as their claims had been ratified by simple tests as satisfying the linguistic and cultural requirements, as most of them were, they became instant citizens, though often unpopular with their new neighbours. The principle of recognition in Germany, as in Israel, is not a cultural one, still less that of birth on the territory: it is primarily that of descent, romanticised as membership of the German people.

To be naturalised as a German citizen, one has to renounce whatever citizenship one then possesses. Turkish and other minorities of people from outside the EU see the recognition of dual citizenship as of greater importance than legislation against racial discrimination. They need German citizenship to obtain the same rights as others living in the country, and to guarantee them against removal; but they need to retain citizenship in the land of their birth, to enable them freely to return if they should choose to do so. The Social Democratic Party promised to legalise dual nationality when it came to power; in the event, when Schröder became Chancellor in October 1998, the naturalisation process was somewhat liberalised, but, owing to xenophobic pressure from the electorate, the bar on dual citizenship remained intact.

Italy sees itself as a country of emigration. In the twentieth century, it has largely been so: Italians have left their country to go, permanently or temporarily, to the United States, Latin America and Australia, and also to other European countries, including Britain, France, Germany and Belgium. Save for a few refugees, there was little immigration into Italy until the late 1970s. Then African immigration, from Somalia and sub-Saharan countries, began on a large scale. As a result, Italy has for the first time become a country of net immigration. Like Spain, Portugal and Greece, Italy makes little distinction between immigrants proper and asylum-seekers; it is next to impossible to get an asylum claim accepted. Until 1989, Italy recognised only east Europeans as refugees.

The increase in immigration, particularly from Africa, has inflamed racist feeling within a sizable section of the Italian population, though not the whole; this effect was exacerbated by the temporary recrudescence of the right before Silvio Berlusconi came to power in March 1994 in alliance with Umberto Bossi's Northern League and the neo-Fascist MSI, led by Gianfranco Fini; Berlusconi himself fell from office in December of that year, and the alliance government survived only until 1996, though now the right is experiencing a resurgence. Fini has repeatedly described Mussolini as the greatest statesman of the century; his MSI, though purporting to be moderate, is frankly racist and against all immigrants, whether from Africa, Russia, Poland or anywhere else. In May 1994 a Fascist demonstration took place in Vicenza; participants wore black shirts,

chanted 'We are the heirs of Salò', referring to the final epi-
sode of Fascist rule in Italy, and tried to set fire to immigrants'
homes. Skinheads from all over Italy took part; they were led by
the head of the youth section of the MSI. The Northern League
purveys what may be called an intra-Italian racism, preaching
hatred of Southerners and calling for the division of the country into two; but when hostility to immigrants began to swell
in the early 1990s, it made that, too, its own, and has voiced
crudely racist statements against African immigrants.

There has been a good deal of racist violence in Italy in recent years; as usual, the Gypsies have suffered the worst of it.
There were repeated attacks in December 1990 on camps accommodating Gypsies in Bologna: cars would drive up, and
from them hooded men would then fire indiscriminately at the
residents.[4] In Pisa, in March 1995, a motorist gave two Gypsy
children a gift-box which then exploded in their faces; one lost
an eye and had to have face and hands reconstructed by plas-
tic surgery; the other lost most of his fingers. Three men were
charged with this revolting crime; all were given suspended
sentences, two of 22 months and one of 8 months. From January 1994 to March 1995 there were more than 125 attacks
on Gypsy camps located in the outskirts of Italian cities, camps
deprived of light, heating or hygienic services because of opposition by right-wing politicians to making them habitable.[5]
In some places the police have taken part in this; in January
1995 police officers in Bologna were convicted of taking part
in a terror campaign against Gypsies, shooting at their caravans
to kill and wound them.[6] The prosecution of those who commit racist crimes is frequently nullified by the derisorily lenient
sentences imposed by the courts. When, in February 1994, a
Tunisian was beaten up on a bus, and, when he got off, chased
by a gang of some fifty skinheads, kicked and stabbed, eleven
youths were arrested and charged with attempted murder.

Their parents are reported to have threatened the police for arresting Italians who were only trying to defend the nation from blacks. They were given suspended sentences of a year and six months. In June three young men were fined and given suspended sentences of a year and eight months when convicted of wounding a Congolese man and of robbing him with violence.[7]

Italian legislation concerning immigration is noteworthy for two characteristics: it is enlightened and humane; and it is flouted and unenforced. The Martelli law, which came into force in 1990, was the first Italian law dealing with immigration and asylum since the Fascist period. It recognised the granting of refugee status to people from outside Europe 'under the warrant of the UN High Commission for Refugees', authorised a 45-day subsistence allowance for asylum-seekers and attempted to reform the process of examining claims for asylum. It also established a new system to govern the entry of ordinary immigrants from outside the EC: they were to apply to the police within eight days of arrival for residence permits, valid for two years and renewable for a further two years on proof of employment and a fixed abode. The law was welcomed by the Left as rescuing people with no secure status from exploitation by unscrupulous employers. It did not work well. Only a very small number of claims for asylum were granted, only a minority of asylum-seekers received the subsistence allowance and the great majority of asylum applications submitted to the police were not forwarded to the Ministry of the Interior for consideration. In 1993 a decree-law, known as the Mancino law, was passed in a hurry, in response to a public outcry about the inhuman conditions under which Somalis were living in Italian cities: this authorised the granting of exceptional leave to remain for refugees from war or from famine, and hence not qualifying as refugees under the narrow definition of the Geneva Convention. Exceptional leave was valid for one year, and gave rights of residence, employment and medical treatment. This contrasts with the constant mouthing by British Labour and Conservative politicians of the prejudicial phrase 'bogus asylum-seekers'. The Mancino law contained strong provisions against racial discrimination and racial violence, and banned organisations dedicated to arousing hatred against racial or religious groups, prescribed stiff prison sentences on individuals for belonging to or assisting them and prohibited the holding of public meetings at which emblems of such hatred were displayed. In 1994 the Ministry of the Interior circularised police stations that residence permits for ordinary immigrants were to be granted for four years, and that proof of employment was no longer required; but this regulation was widely flouted by the police. The Fascist rally of 1994 at Vicenza plainly contravened this law, yet the police did nothing to interfere with it; the same holds good of other subsequent meetings. In general, the Mancino law has simply not been applied.

With the exception of Luxembourg, Europe's most tolerant country, where 25 per cent of the workforce is made up of immigrants, all European countries have experienced a rising level of racism in the past decade, combated, with greater or less effectiveness, by dedicated opponents. This racism has been manifested by frightening violence against ethnic minorities, and has been incorporated into the programmes of right-wing political parties, pressure from which has influenced the policies of mainstream parties. It was remarked above that the heated national debate on the number of refugees entering the country that took place in Germany in 1991 bore fruit in the disgusting attack on a hostel for refugees in Hoyerswerda, followed by arson attacks in 1992 and 1993. From that point on, the level of violence against racial minorities throughout Germany has remained extremely high; for instance, in August 1999 five youths in Eggesin, near the Polish frontier, set on two Vietnamese, beat them into unconsciousness and continued to kick them with their boots; they were sentenced to between four and six years' imprisonment for attempted murder.[8] In Berlin and Hamburg the police themselves have been accused of being implicated in some racial crimes. In El Ejido in Spain violent riots directed at Moroccan workers erupted in early February 2000, and a number of arson attacks on them were perpetrated there in April.[9] In February 1990 two hundred people, armed with iron bars and baseball bats, carried out an organised beating of black people and Gypsies in the city centre of Florence; racist violence has been a feature of Italian life ever since.[10] Violent expression of racial prejudice goes back to 1973 in France; in that year there was an outburst of violence in Marseilles, principally directed against Algerians, which then spread to other French cities. There is still a high level of racism among the white French population. There have been numerous racist murders, mostly of North Africans,[11] and of course insults and lesser violence. The level of discrimination is high, both in employment and in public places, particularly discothèques and also bars and cafés. In questionnaires, large number of respondents do not hesitate to identify themselves as racist. Racial violence is not confined to EU countries: from June to September 1991 there were at least fifteen attacks in several Swiss towns and cities against centres accommodating foreigners.[12]

It should be obvious that if there is to be control of immigration from outside the European Union into countries that are members of it, and scrutiny of claims for admission and the grant of refugee status, these ought both to be administered by authorities of the Union, rather than by those of individual member states. Free movement within the European Community has been one of its objectives ever since its foundation, though resisted by Britain; but this at present is the right only of those holding the European citizenship conferred by the Maastricht Treaty on nationals of member states. It needs to be extended to nationals of other ('third') countries lawfully living in the Union, just as it is accepted that, within any one country, anyone, whether citizen or not, may freely travel from one place to another. The principle of free movement within Europe can hardly be workable unless there is a unified system supervising movement into it.

The arrival of refugees – strictly to be distinguished from ordinary immigrants – is unpredictable, depending on conflicts, acts of repression and disasters occurring elsewhere. There cannot therefore be a policy regulating their arrival; but there ought to be an agreement over what constitutes a valid claim for admission, and arrangements to allocate those granted asylum to member states best able to accommodate them. Inflows of immigrants properly so called are more easily regulated; and for demographic reasons Europe may well soon stand in need of immigration on a substantial scale. The EU, often the goal of many suffering from intolerable poverty, ought to operate a humane policy, in which the claim to family unity plays a salient role; it can best do so if it adopts an immigration policy for the Union as a whole, rather than leaving each member state to devise its own. Several vague aspirations to a common immigration and asylum policy have been expressed, but nothing concrete results. The principal reason for this is the attitude of politicians in the various individual countries, determined to keep immigration control in the hands of national governments. They speak of national sovereignty, but their main motive is to avoid the leniency which they fear from a policy administered by the Union. The administration of a common immigration policy must be based as far as possible on objective criteria, rather than on the discretion of officials. A wide latitude given to their discretion leads to injustice and arbitrary decisions; they are subject to political pressure and influenced by public sentiment. The most important objective criterion is the need to preserve family unity. Another is ill treatment in the home country, not sufficient for a claim to asylum, but establishing a humanitarian ground for emigration. The needs of member states, such as a general labour shortage or a dearth of people with particular skills, plainly furnish other criteria. The ideal is to enshrine such criteria in definite rights that intending immigrants can claim.

The Maastricht Treaty of 1991 founded the European Union upon three 'pillars', the first being the agencies of the European Community, the second inter-governmental cooperation on a common foreign and security policy, and the third cooperation between governments on matters of justice and home affairs. Cooperation under the third pillar concentrated on asylum, border controls, family reunion and illegal immigration; it produced many non-binding documents, but did not succeed in harmonising immigration and asylum policies. The Amsterdam Treaty, which came into force in May 1999, inserted an Article 13 into the Treaty establishing the European Community, allowing Community institutions to adopt measures against racial, religious or other forms of discrimination. It also added a new Title IV on immigration and asylum to that Treaty, thereby transferring questions concerning them from the third to the first pillar; but the UK, Ireland and Denmark have reserved the right not to be bound by measures adopted by the Council of Ministers under Title IV, and to take no part in the process of adopting them. For five years at least, legislative proposals under Title IV may be made not only by the European Commission, but also by the governments of member states; measures will be adopted only by unanimous approval.[13] It is evident that this may lead to paralysis.

A Plan of Action was formulated, requiring the adoption within two years of measures on the status of legal immigrants, readmission, visas, carriers' liability and the repression of illegal immigration. Five years are allowed for measures on residence permits, conditions of entry and the right (if any) of nationals of countries not in the EU legally resident in one member state to reside in another.

A European Council meeting in Tampere in October 1999 considered immigration and refugees. It came forward with some pious hopes, but little commitment to definite action. It recommended consultation with sending countries, encouraging them to combat poverty and respect human rights. It advocated a common European asylum system in the long term, and demanded respect for the right to seek asylum. Non-citizens of the EU legally residing within member states were to have rights and obligations 'comparable to' those of EU citizens; a draft urging that they have the same rights and obligations is believed to have been rejected at the instance of Austria. There should be a common policy on visas; illegal immigration was to be tackled at source, and severe sanctions imposed for trafficking in human beings. Expressed in those words, this indeed sounds a horrible crime; when means of escape are blocked and borders all but closed, such traffickers supply almost the only way in which the persecuted and desperate can reach possible sanctuaries. The French Prime Minister responded by declaring that decisions on asylum should remain within national competence; the consensus in Britain that both asylum and immigration should be regulated solely by the national government is well known.

It seems questionable whether the aspirations voiced at Tampere will ever be realised. However, in November 1999 the European Commission published three proposals to combat racial discrimination under Article 13 of the Amsterdam Treaty.

These proposals were: (i) for a directive requiring member states to render unlawful discrimination in employment or training on grounds of race, ethnic origin, religion, disability, age or sexual orientation; (ii) another directive requiring member states to render unlawful discrimination in any area of life directed against any, whether EU citizens or third-country nationals, on grounds of race or ethnic origin; and (iii) an action programme, to run from 2001 to 2006, to fund practical action by member states to promote racial equality in all areas covered by either directive. If these proposals are adopted, a big step will have been taken towards implementing Article 13.

Diverse currents swirl about Europe: currents of panic, cruelty and hatred; a strong current of obtuse selfishness, oblivious to its likely consequences; and a current of sanity and humanity. Only if this last predominates will there be hope of averting disaster for the world outside Europe and within it.

NOTES

1 Colette Smith, 'Lyons', in Ann Dummett (ed.), *Racially Motivated Crime*, Commission for Racial Equality, London, 1997, pp. 81–2.

2 *Migration News Sheet* for March 2000, p. 14. The issue for January 1994 had stated on p. 9 that the Czech Interior Ministry had reported 94 attacks against Roma since 1991, in which sixteen of the victims had been killed.

3 *Migration News Sheet* for June 1993, pp. 9–10, quoting *Süddeutsche Zeitung*, 6, 30 and 31 May 1993, and for July 1993, pp. 8–9, quoting *Süddeutsche Zeitung*, 4, 5, 8 and 17 June 1993.

4 *Migration News Sheet* for January 1991, p. 11, quoting *Corriere della Sera*, 12 December 1990, and *Il Messagero*, 24 December 1990.

5 See Jolanda Chirico, 'Rome', in Ann Dummett (ed.), *Racially Motivated Crime*, CRE, London, 1997, p. 113.

6 Ibid., p. 119.

7 Ibid., pp. 120–2.

8 *Migration News Sheet* for May 2000, p. 16.

9 *Migration News Sheet* for March 2000, pp. 14–15, and for May 2000, p. 16.

10 Jolanda Chirico, 'Rome', in Ann Dummett (ed.), *Racially Motivated Crime*, CRE, London, 1997, p. 99.

11 See *Migration News Sheet* for March 1995, p. 9, June 1995, p. 9, March 1996, p. 13, April 1996, p. 12, July 1997, p. 13, January 1998, p. 13, and June 1998, p. 16.

12 *Migration News Sheet* for October 1991, pp. 11–12, quoting *24 Heures*, 18 September 1991, and *La Suisse*, 14 September 1991.

13 See Jan Niessen, *EU Policies on Immigration and Integration after the Amsterdam Treaty*, FORUM and the Migration Policy Group, Utrecht, 1999.

INDEX

Note: Page numbers followed by "n" denote endnotes.

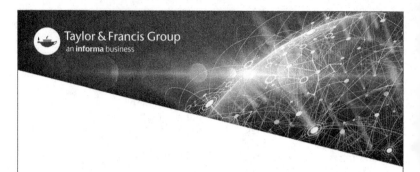

Printed in the United States
by Baker & Taylor Publisher Services